STOP THE SALT

Low Sodium Cooking For One Without Killing Yourself

Steve Cooper
@coopertalk

STOP THE SALT

Copyright © 2015

All rights reserved. No part of this book may be reproduced by any means whatsoever without the written permission of the author, except for very brief portions of the book which may be quoted for the purpose of review.

The information presented within this book has been carefully researched and checked for factual accuracy. Nonetheless, the author and publisher make no warrantee; either express or implied, that the information contained herein is appropriate to every individual, situation and purpose, and assume no responsibility for errors or omissions. The reader assumes the risk and full responsibility for his or her actions, and the author and publisher will not be held responsible for any loss or damage, whether such loss or damage be consequential, incidental, special or otherwise, that may result from the information presented in this book.

The author has relied upon many sources, and his own experience, in compiling this book and has done his very best to check facts and to give credit where credit is due. Should any of the material contained in this book be inaccurate, or have been used without the proper permissions, please contact the author so that any oversight may be corrected.

Table of Contents

INTRODUCTION 1
DINNER TIME 5
SAMMIES & SUCH 49
PASTARAMA AND OTHER HITS 83
SOME SALADS & SOME SIDES 103

STOP THE SALT

INTRODUCTION

A couple of years ago I was diagnosed with Congestive Heart Failure. I wasn't overweight, I was somewhat healthy, but yet I had this condition. Well, I take that back, I wasn't that healthy, but looked like I was in good shape. I smoked, drank lots of coffee and had a bad diet. In the past I had been a Stand-Up Comic on the road and then worked in many different facets of the Restaurant business, so basically I didn't eat healthy. It may have been through laziness or that I just didn't really take the time to cook, but the bottom line, my diet and lifestyle was a time bomb waiting to go off.

The bomb went off one day. I had been feeling terrible for weeks. During that time I learned the difference between being tired and being exhausted. Being tired is, "I don't want to get out of bed. I want to sleep a little more". Being exhausted is, "I can't get out of bed. I don't have the physical strength to do anything". This went on until I couldn't take it anymore. I went to the Emergency Room and was admitted.

The Doctors first thought it was walking pneumonia because I had fluid in my chest, but then it turned out to be the dreaded CHF. In shock, I thought to myself that I was going to have to get opened up but I soon learned that wasn't the case. To control the fluid I had to cut down on my Sodium intake.

Sodium is a killer and is ignored all the time. If you eat in fast food establishments at other restaurants or enjoy processed food you are subjecting yourself to high sodium counts. (I did all of those things.) Food companies advertise their product as low in calories but never mention how much sodium is in it.

At first the change in my diet was intimidating. I knew how to cook but didn't do it much. (And people always say that cooking for one is so expensive.) It turned out to be very easy and to be honest, if you shopped smart, it was pretty cheap. I started cooking at home and figuring out cool ways to create dishes. Shopping was now an experience for me.

STOP THE SALT

Checking prices and monitoring sodium levels was like a hobby. (My friend who is a Manager at a big Grocery Store in LA was surprised that I knew what was on sale at not only his chain but every other one around town.)

I soon started eating healthy and noticed a change. My blood pressure lowered, I didn't have any trouble breathing or have tightness in my chest and could feel myself getting healthier. My Cardiologist was impressed by my progress and I vowed to stay healthy. (Of course I gave up cigarettes too and if you are a smoker, please stop.)

I continue to make progress and decided to write this book. I'm not saying to never eat fast food or junk food again because it is a guilty pleasure. I'm also not saying to never go to a nice eatery or chain restaurant either. I'm just saying, start cooking at home and watching the sodium. You will notice the difference.

KEY

One of the reasons why people are so intimidated by cooking is because the recipes have so many ingredients and instructions. At times they seem harder to understand than the directions for Ikea furniture. So I have decided to make it easy for you, because that is one of the main reasons you purchased this book, so you can whip up a meal and not think too much about it.

For every recipe you will use the following measurements for sides and vegetables unless directed differently by the recipe. This way there is no need to worry and everything is uniform.

VEGETABLES:

For veggies that are one piece, for example, Zucchini, Squash, Peppers and others it will be exactly that, one piece. (I usually weigh them so they are around ½ pound.)

For veggies that are many pieces, for example, Green Beans, Broccoli, Asparagus and others it will be exactly that, many pieces. (Once again, go for a ½ pound.)

When cooking your veggies, first you will clean them up and then microwave them unless of course directed differently. This process will be, putting them in a microwave safe container, add a little bit of water and cover the bowl. You will then microwave them on high for 3½–5 minutes. (The time will depend on the power of your microwave and your desired crispness. I like my veggies softer while my girlfriend likes hers with more of a snap.)

GRAINS AND SUCH:

This category includes the sides that are included in my recipes that will make your meal balanced and your plate sexy. At times depending on your mood, you can skip these and go all veggies. Sides I like are Quinoa, Pasta, Rice and Couscous but you can explore others. All of these will be cooked by following the directions on the box. It's that easy. My suggested serving size differs from the box, because they tend to be on the small side. I suggest ⅓ cup of Quinoa and ½ cup for the Rice, Pasta and Couscous. (When these grains are used for the main course, portions will be bigger and noted.)

POTATOES:

Potatoes can be a good addition to a meal. The types I use in the book are Russet, Ruby Gold or Baby Red Potatoes. Once again go for the ½ pound rule.

When cooking once again it depends on your microwave. Make sure you poke some holes in the potato after washing it. Then put it on a microwave safe plate that has a sheet of paper towel on it. Microwave on high for 5 – 7 minutes or until a fork can easily slide into it.

MEATS:

All steak, pork, chicken, fish and other types of meat will also follow the ½ pound rule. They will be cooked according to what the different recipes call for. (Oven will always be preheated at 400 degrees.)

One of the complaints people have about eating healthy is that it is too expensive. For some reason they think it is cheaper to go grab Fast Food. It isn't. (Unless of course you are eating off the dollar menu, but just think of the quality of food you get with that.)

To help make this book work you will have to shop. Yes, it sounds like a scary task for you newbies, but it isn't. You will find that after a while you will start to dig the whole process which includes label reading. You are going to need to check for sodium content and in time you won't believe how much of it is in products that you swore were good for you.

Also remember, Grocery Store Club Cards are your friend. Buy what is on special so you can save a few bucks. When it comes to meats and fish, find a good sale and buy two pounds and freeze them. (Most butchers will gladly cut your purchase into those ½ pound sizes that you will be eating.)

DINNER TIME

STOP THE SALT

OUT OF THE CAN FIESTA PORK AND BEANS

Did you know that commercially canned pork and beans were introduced in the United States during the 1880s? The dish is "an American canned classic, and is recognized by consumers generally as an item that contains very little pork." This is due to the high fat content of the salt pork traditionally used in American pork and beans, which often renders into solution when sufficiently heated.

That's the canned stuff that is loaded with sodium. This recipe is a much healthier version with a Southwestern flare!

INGREDIENTS

Boneless Pork Chop
Black Pepper
Olive Oil
¼ can of Low Sodium Black Beans, with liquid
¼ cup of Low Sodium Salsa
Brown Rice
Green Peppers

DIRECTIONS

Pepper the Pork Chop to your liking. Heat desired amount of Olive Oil in frying pan over medium-high heat. Brown Chop on both sides.

Pour undrained Beans and Salsa over Pork Chop. Bring liquid to a boil then reduce heat to medium-low and cover. Simmer for between 20-35 minutes until pork is cooked through. (If you're worried, cut open to make sure there is no pink.)

Serve with Brown Rice and Green Pepper. (Slice Pepper into small pieces and mix into Rice.)

ITALIAN CATFISH (NO WHISKERS)

The Catfish is a freshwater fish which is named after the barbells around its mouth that resembles the whiskers of a cat. There are thousands of known species of catfish, and some of them don't even have the whisker-shaped barrels on their mouths. Catfishes are characterized by a forked or ray-shaped tails and a silvery blue or light olive body which is covered with black spots. They are also considered as game fish because they are quick and precise swimmers.

INGREDIENTS

Catfish Fillet
½ tablespoon Lemon Juice
¼ teaspoon Pepper
⅛ cup Lower Sodium Parmesan Cheese
1 tablespoon Unsalted Butter
¾ tablespoon Low Fat Mayonnaise
1 Roma Tomato sliced thin

DIRECTIONS

Preheat Broiler. Coat a Cooking Pan with Nonstick Cooking Spray. Brush both sides of Catfish with Lemon Juice and then sprinkle with Pepper. Place fish on pan.

In a small bowl, mix Parmesan Cheese, Butter and Mayonnaise.

Broil fish for 8 minutes. Remove pan and turn fish over. Spread the Cheese Mixture over that side of the Fillet. Top with Tomato Slices. Broil 8 more minutes or until Fish flakes with fork.

Serve with Quinoa and Asparagus.

STOP THE SALT

PEPPERED PERKY PREPARED PERCH

That's a lot of P's. Did you know the common and yellow perches are found, respectively, in the fresh waters of Eurasia and North America? Both are well-known and popular as both food and sport fishes. They have two dorsal fins, the first spiny and the second soft-rayed.

And wherever they are from, one thing is for sure, they are tasty! But ignore them as a sport fish, because they look better on your plate then hanging on your wall.

INGREDIENTS

Perch Fillets
½ cup Flour
½ teaspoon Black Pepper
½ teaspoon Cayenne Pepper
1 tablespoon Unsalted Butter
½ Lemon

DIRECTIONS

Mix together Flour, Black Pepper and Cayenne Pepper in a bowl. Press Perch into mixture to coat.

Heat butter in Frying Pan over medium heat until it is foaming. Place Perch in pan and cook until golden. (About 4 minutes each side.)

Place Fillets on plate and squeeze lemon juice over them.

Serve on top of White Rice with sliced Zucchini.

TILAPIA PARMESAN NOT PARMIGIANA

Just so you know this dish in nothing like Veal or Chicken Parmigiana, but still is excellent. Tilapia is the common name for nearly a hundred species of cichlid fish from the tilapiine cichlid tribe. Tilapia are mainly freshwater fish, inhabiting shallow streams, ponds, rivers and lakes, and less commonly found living in brackish water. Historically, they have been of major importance in artisan fishing in Africa and the Levant, and are of increasing importance in aquaculture.

INGREDIENTS

Tilapia fillets
1 tablespoon Low Fat Mayonnaise
¼ cup Panko Bread Crumbs
1 tablespoon Parmesan Cheese
Black Pepper
Dried Basil

DIRECTIONS

Preheat oven. Coat a Cooking Pan with Nonstick Cooking Spray.

In a small bowl mix Bread Crumbs, Parmesan Cheese and a few shakes of Basil and Black Pepper.

Lightly spread Mayo on the Tilapia Fillets and then coat the Fish with Bread Crumb mixture.

Bake 20-25 minutes until desired consistency.

Serve with Cous Cous and Broccoli.

STOP THE SALT

NOT A LOUISIANA SHRIMP BOIL (BURL)... UNLESS YOU'RE IN LOUISIANA

You might want to put a little Zydeco music on and speak with a Creole draw when preparing this dish. Seafood boil is the generic term for any number of different kinds of social events in which shellfish is the central element. Regional variations dictate the kinds of seafood, the accompaniments and side dishes, and the preparation techniques (boiling, steaming, baking, or raw). In some cases, a boil may be sponsored by a community organization as a fund-raiser or a mixer. Today, however, we are going Louisiana!

INGREDIENTS

½ pound Shrimp
1 ear of Corn
½ pound Baby Red Potatoes
2 Garlic Cloves
¼ Yellow Onion
½ Lemon
Tabasco
Crushed Red Pepper

DIRECTIONS

Fill a 6 quart pot half way with water and start to boil. Peel Shrimp, shuck Corn and cut into three pieces, quarter Red Potatoes, slice Garlic thinly, and cut Yellow Onion into wedges.

As water is coming to a boil add a few shakes of Tabasco and Red Pepper. Then squeeze juice from Lemon into the water and then drop it in. Add Garlic and Onion.

Let INGREDIENTS boil together for a few minutes then add Potatoes. Boil for 10 minutes.

Add Corn and continue to boil for 5 more minutes.

Toss in Shrimp and cover pot. (Only have lid cover ¾ so steam can escape.) Boil for 3 minutes.

Remove pot from stove and pour through pasta strainer and remove lemon.

Serve in Pasta Bowl or large Plate.

TIME FOR ME TO SWAI

Yes, a lame REO Speedwagon reference, but don't judge. So what is Swai? It is similar to catfish with its white flesh, but has a milder flavor and more delicate texture. This fish is from Vietnam and brings a moist, sweet taste to your tongue with a coarser texture to break up the sometimes perceived "slimy" feel of fish. It has a very approachable flavor for most people who don't normally like freshwater fish.

INGREDIENTS

Swai Fillet
Asparagus
Black Pepper
Lemon
Olive Oil
No Sodium Original Blend Seasoning

DIRECTIONS

Preheat oven. Put a good amount of foil on a Cooking Pan and coat with Nonstick Cooking Spray.

Lay Asparagus on foil and brush with Olive Oil and sprinkle Original Blend Seasoning.

Place Swai on top of Asparagus. Brush with Olive Oil and then squeeze Lemon on Fish and add Crushed Black Pepper to taste.

Wrap up foil around Fish and Asparagus so it forms a pouch and encases the food.

Cook for 25 minutes.

Remove from oven, open foil and plate Fish and Asparagus. Serve with White Rice.

STOP THE SALT

HAMBURGER ENABLER

Just so you know, I'm not making fun of Hamburger Helper. I love that stuff, except for the sodium content. (And to be honest, that Mascot Hand they use, creeps me out just a little.) Did you know the pasta and seasoning mix known as 'Hamburger Helper' was introduced in 1970 by General Mills. The product was created during a meat shortage, and was designed to help housewives stretch a pound of ground beef (hamburger) into a tasty family meal. It was a huge success and other versions, including Tuna Helper, were later introduced. Well now I introduce my version.

INGREDIENTS

Lean Ground Beef or Turkey
1 cup Large Elbow Macaroni
Olive Oil
¼ cup Low Sodium Tomato Sauce
¼ Yellow Onion
Crushed Red Pepper
or
No Sodium Extra Spicy Seasoning

DIRECTIONS

Prepare Macaroni.

Pour some Olive Oil in a Frying Pan and add meat, cooking over medium heat. Stir in Crushed Red Pepper or Spicy Seasoning to your taste preference.

Chop onion finely into very small pieces and add to meat.

As meat is near being finished, put Tomato Sauce in Microwave Safe Bowl and cover with plastic. Cook on High for 3 – 5 minutes. (Depending on power of Microwave.)

Drain Pasta and put back in pot. Drain Meat and Onion Mixture.

Add mixture and sauce to pasta, toss and serve in a bowl or on a plate.

SORT OF SUCCOTASH

Sylvester the Cat used to say, "Suffering Succotash" and I have no idea why. (In fact Daffy Duck ripped the line off a few times to.) Succotash is a food dish consisting primarily of corn and lima beans or other shell beans. Other ingredients may be added including tomatoes and green or sweet red peppers. Because of the relatively inexpensive and more readily available ingredients, the dish was popular during the Great Depression in the United States. The Native Americans in the eastern woodlands were the first to prepare this dish.

INGREDIENTS

Boneless Skinless Chicken Breast
¼ small Onion
½ Zucchini
½ cup thawed Frozen Corn
8 ounces Low Sodium Diced Tomato with Juice
1 teaspoon Chili Powder
Black Pepper
Olive Oil
White Rice

DIRECTIONS

Heat Olive Oil on medium in Frying Pan. Add Chicken and cover. Cook for 3 minutes, flip and cook for 3 more. Remove chicken and cut into small cubes.

Chop Onion and slice Zucchini. (Cut into thin medallion shape and then cut that four ways.)

Put a little more Oil in Pan. Cook Onion 4 minutes then add Zucchini and cook 2 minutes.

Add Tomatoes with their Juice, Corn, Chili Powder and Ground Black Pepper and stir.

Bring to a boil over high heat, reduce heat and simmer 5 minutes.

Stir in Chicken and cook 5 minutes or until it is done and Veggies are tender.

Serve over White Rice.

STOP THE SALT

COD DARN THAT'S GOOD

Cod is mostly associated with Fish and Chips or for being fried, but it is good without the batter. The Atlantic Cod will actually change colors depending on which depth they are hanging around at and will typically be a grey-green color or a lovely reddish-brown color. Years ago, every now and again, a Cod would be found that had a deformed head, which looked very much like the crown of a king. Naturally, these fish became known as King Cod and at one point in time, Norwegians believed they could use them to predict the weather.

INGREDIENTS

Cod Fillet
½ Orange
½ Lemon
1 tablespoon Green Onions
Black Pepper

DIRECTIONS

Preheat Broiler. Put foil on a Cooking Pan and coat with Nonstick Cooking Spray.

Combine juice of Orange and Lemon with Black Pepper in a bowl. Mix and let sit for 5 minutes.

Place Fillet on Cooking Pan and broil for 8-10 minutes or until it flakes.

Slice Green Onions and when Fish is plated top it with them.

Serve with Brussels Sprouts and Farro. (Squeeze juice from other ½ of Lemon on Brussel Sprouts.)

SOMBRERO CHICKEN

Salsa is for more than just chips, even though it is awesome on chips. Salsa can be traced to the Aztecs, Mayans and Incas. The Spaniards first encountered tomatoes after their conquest of Mexico in 1519-1521, which marked the beginning of the history of Salsa sauce. Aztec lords combined tomatoes with chili peppers, ground squash seeds and consumed them mainly as a condiment served on turkey, venison, lobster, and fish. This combination was subsequently called salsa by Alonso de Molina in 1571.

INGREDIENTS

Chicken Breast
¼ cup Low Sodium Salsa
½ Jalapeno Pepper, sliced
5 small Black Olives, halved

DIRECTIONS

Preheat oven.

Put large piece of foil on Cooking Pan.

Place chicken on foil and pour salsa over it.

Place peppers and olives on chicken.

Wrap it up in the foil.

Bake for 40 minutes.

Serve with Green Peppers and Brown and White Rice mixture.

SNAPPER...I HARDLY EVEN KNOW HER

When I refer to Snapper, I'm not talking about those Turtles that would always steal my bait when fishing in my youth. I'm talking Red Snapper. In Latin American Spanish it is known as huachinango or pargo. All feature a sloped profile, medium-to-large scales, a spiny dorsal fin and a laterally compressed body. The maximum published age of a caught red snapper was reported to be 57 years. Coloration of the red snapper is light red, with more intense pigment on the back. A red snapper attains sexual maturity at two to five years old and an adult snapper can live for more than 50 years and weigh 50 pounds.

INGREDIENTS

Red Snapper fillet
¼ Yellow Onion, sliced thin
½ Red Pepper, sliced thin
½ cup Pre-Sliced Mushroom
2 teaspoon No Sodium Original Seasoning
½ Lemon

DIRECTIONS

Preheat oven.

In a small bowl mix onion, red pepper, mushrooms and seasoning.

Put a good amount of foil on a Cooking Pan and coat with Nonstick Cooking Spray.

Place Red Snapper on foil. Top with veggie mixture. Squeeze juice of the lemon over it.

Wrap up in foil and cook for 20 minutes.

Serve with Green Beans and Cous Cous.

HONEY CHOP

Honey collection is an ancient activity. Humans began hunting for honey at least 8,000 years ago, as evidenced by a cave painting in Valencia, Spain. The painting is a Mesolithic rock painting, showing two honey-hunters collecting honey and honeycomb from a wild bee nest. The figures are depicted carrying baskets or gourds, and using a ladder or series of ropes to reach the wild nest. Thanks to them, we can now make this great recipe.

INGREDIENTS

1 Pork Chop
2 tablespoons Honey
1½ tablespoons Dijon or Spicy Mustard
⅓ cup Low Sodium Chicken Broth
1 teaspoon Garlic Powder
1 teaspoon Dried Basil

DIRECTIONS

Preheat Oven.

Combine all **INGREDIENTS**, except pork chops in a baking dish and mix well.

Add Pork and cover. Bake for 20 minutes.

Uncover and cook for 10 more minutes.

Serve with Brussels Sprouts and Baby Red Potatoes.

PORKY AND TOM TOM

Botanically, a tomato is a fruit. However, the tomato has a much lower sugar content than other edible fruits, and is therefore not as sweet. Typically served as part of a salad or main course of a meal, rather than at dessert, it is considered a vegetable for most culinary uses. One exception is that tomatoes are treated as a fruit in home canning practices and are processed in a water bath rather than a pressure cooker as vegetables would require. Tomatoes are not the only food source with this ambiguity: green beans, eggplants, cucumbers, and squashes of all kinds are all botanically fruits, yet cooked as vegetables.

INGREDIENTS

1 Pork Chop
¼ Large Onion, thinly sliced
¼ pint Red Grape Tomatoes, halved
1 clove Garlic, diced
1 ounce Crumbled Feta Cheese
Black Pepper
1 teaspoon Dried Basil

DIRECTIONS

Heat Olive Oil is pan over medium heat. Add onion and cook until golden. Set aside.

Season Pork Chop with Black Pepper.

Add more Olive Oil to pan and add Pork Chop. Cook 10-15 minutes until done. Set aside.

Add even more Olive Oil to pan. Return Onion and stir in Tomatoes, Garlic and Basil. Cook for about 3 minutes until Tomatoes are tender.

Top Pork Chop with mixture and sprinkle Feta Cheese on top.

Serve with Asparagus and Cous Cous.

EASY THERE MR. AHI

Just so you know, technically it is called Yellowfin Tuna and just marketed as Ahi. The species name, albacares (white meat) can also lead to confusion. In English, the albacore tuna (Thunnus alalunga) is a different species. Yellowfin are able to escape most of predators, because unlike most fish, tuna are warm-blooded, and their warm muscles make them incredibly strong swimmers, with yellowfin tuna reaching speeds of up to 50 miles per hour.

INGREDIENTS

Ahi Tuna
Olive Oil
Black Pepper

DIRECTIONS

Heat up Pan to medium to high heat.

Brush Ahi with Olive Oil and give a nice coating of Black Pepper.

Place Ahi in pan and cover with a lid. Cook for 4 minutes.

Flip and cook the other side covered for 4 minutes or until outside is crusted.

Serve with Asparagus and Quinoa.

NUTTY FISH

Did you know that Pecans contain more than 19 vitamins and minerals? Which include vitamin A, vitamin E, folic acid, calcium, magnesium, phosphorus, potassium, several B vitamins and zinc. One ounce of pecans provides 10 percent of the recommended Daily Value for fiber. Pecans are also a natural, high-quality source of protein that are naturally sodium-free, making them an excellent choice for this dish.

INGREDIENTS

Tilapia
½ ounce of ground Pecans
½ tablespoon Parsley
Dash of Cayenne

DIRECTIONS

Preheat Oven. Coat a Cooking Pan with Nonstick Cooking Spray.

In a small bowl mix together Pecans, Parsley and Cayenne.

Using your fingertips gently press this mixture on the Tilapia until it sticks.

Bake 20 minutes until it flakes.

Serve with White Rice and Green Beans.

CHICKEN SPROUT

Production of Brussels Sprouts in the United States began in the 18th century, when French settlers brought them to Louisiana. Thomas Jefferson grew them at Monticello. The first plantings in California's Central Coast began in the 1920s, with significant production beginning in the 1940s. Currently, several thousand acres are planted in coastal areas of San Mateo, Santa Cruz, and Monterey Counties of California, which offer an ideal combination of coastal fog and cool temperatures year-round. The harvest season lasts from June through January. They are also grown in Baja California, Mexico, where the harvest season is from December through June.

INGREDIENTS

Bone-In Chicken, drumsticks
Brussels Sprouts
Olive Oil
2 teaspoons Low Sodium Mustard
Panko Breadcrumbs
Black Pepper

DIRECTIONS

Preheat oven and spray two Cooking Dishes with Non-Stick Olive Oil spray.

Toss Brussels Sprouts in Olive Oil and Black Pepper and place in one dish.

Coat Drumsticks with Mustard and roll in Breadcrumbs and place in other dish.

Bake both dishes for 30 minutes, turning chicken once and tossing Brussels once halfway.

Serve with Baby Red Potatoes.

STOP THE SALT

THIGH GUY

All parts of the Chicken are good for you, but here are some quick cool facts for you. A. Chickens are pretty fast. The chicken can travel up to 9 miles per hour when it wants to. B. There are more chickens on Earth than there are humans. C. The chicken is the closest living relative of the Tyrannosaurus-Rex. D. There are more chickens on Earth than there are humans. See that? And you thought this book was just recipes.

INGREDIENTS

Boneless, Skinless Chicken Thighs
½ Red Bell Pepper, seeded and cut into slices
½ Medium Red Onion, finely chopped
1 small Zucchini, cut into ½ inch slices
1 tablespoon Olive Oil
1 tablespoon Lemon Juice
1 tablespoon Garlic Powder
1 tablespoon Paprika
Black Pepper

DIRECTIONS

Preheat Oven.

Put Aluminum Foil on Cooking and spray with Nonstick Cooking Spray.

In a large bowl, mix Olive Oil, Lemon Juice, Garlic Powder, Paprika and Black Pepper.

Add Chicken, Pepper, Onion and Zucchini and mix well.

Put Chicken mixture on the Aluminum Foil and wrap tightly.

Cook for 25 minutes.

Serve on top of White Rice.

SORT OF FISH AND CHIPS

Fish and chips became a stock meal among the working classes in Great Britain as a consequence of the rapid development of trawl fishing in the North Sea, and the development of railways which connected the ports to major industrial cities during the second half of the 19th century. Deep-fried fish was first introduced into Britain during the 17th century by Jewish refugees from Portugal and Spain and is derived from Pescado Frito. In 1860, the first fish and chip shop was opened in London by Joseph Malin.

INGREDIENTS

Cod
Zucchini, sliced into thin coin shaped pieces
Olive Oil
Panko Bread Crumbs

DIRECTIONS

Preheat Oven.

Place Aluminum Foil on Tray and spray with Non-Stick Olive Oil Cooking Spray.

Coat Cod and Zucchini with Olive Oil.

Place in Zip Lock bag containing Bread Crumbs and shake until coated.

Place on foil.

Cook for 20 minutes, turning over once.

Remove from oven and plate.

STOP THE SALT

MAN OF STEELHEAD TROUT

Up in the sky, look! It's a bird. It's a plane. It's Superman! No, not really. It's a fish. The rainbow trout is a species of salmonid native to tributaries of the Pacific Ocean in Asia and North America. The steelhead is a sea-run rainbow trout (anadromous) usually returning to freshwater to spawn after two to three years at sea; rainbow trout and steelhead trout are the same species. Several other fish in the salmonid family are called trout; some are anadromous like salmon, whereas others are resident in freshwater only.

INGREDIENTS

Steelhead Trout fillet
Yellow Squash, cut into ½ inch coin shaped pieces
¼ Lemon
Olive Oil
Black Pepper
Cayenne Pepper
Paprika

DIRECTIONS

Put Aluminum Foil on Cooking and spray with Nonstick Olive Oil Cooking Spray.

Place Squash on foil and spray with Cooking Spray. Sprinkle with Paprika.

Put Trout on top of Squash.

Drizzle Trout with Olive Oil and brush until top is coated.

Top with Juice of Lemon, Black Pepper and Cayenne.

Wrap in Aluminum Foil tightly.

Cook 20 minutes and remove from oven.

Serve with Cous Cous.

CILANTRO-LIME TOUGHY ROUGHY

The Orange Roughy is not a vertically slender fish. They turn orange after death, but are red while living. The maximum published age of 149 years was determined via radiometric dating of trace isotopes found in an Orange Roughy's otolith ("ear bone"). Similarly, counting by the growth rings of Orange Roughy otoliths has given a maximum age of 125 to 156 years. The validity of these results is questioned by commercial fishers as some state the former method is controversial and the latter method is known to underestimate age in older specimens.

INGREDIENTS

Orange Roughy Filet
Spinach, cooked
1 Roma Tomato, chopped
Garlic Powder, dash
Olive Oil
Juice of ½ a Lime
1 tablespoon Cilantro

DIRECTIONS

Preheat Broiler.

Brush Olive Oil on Orange Roughy.

Squeeze on Lime Juice and sprinkle with Garlic Powder and Cilantro.

Place on Cooking Tray for 10 minutes or until the fish flakes.

Put Spinach on plate. Place fish on it and top with the chopped Tomatoes.

Serve with Quinoa.

KABOB…SHHHH!

Some call them Kabobs and some call them Kebabs. In English, *kebab* with no qualification generally refers more specifically to shish kebab cooked on a skewer. In the Middle East, however, kebab refers to meat that is cooked over or next to flames; large or small cuts of meat, or even ground meat; it may be served on plates, in sandwiches, or in bowls. Like other ethnic foods brought by travelers, the kebab has become a part of everyday cuisine in many countries.

INGREDIENTS

4 Cremini Mushrooms
¼ Red Onion, cut into 4 chunks
4 Grape or Cherry Tomatoes
⅓ medium Zucchini, halved and cut into 4 slices
½ small Yellow Bell Pepper, halved, seeded and cut into 4 square pieces.
Olive Oil
Oregano

DIRECTIONS

Preheat oven.

Skewer the Vegetables on 4 skewers and place in a baking dish.

Drizzle Olive Oil over them and add Oregano. Toss to coat.

Cover and refrigerate for an hour.

Bake for 15-20 minutes until slightly browned.

Serve on a bed of Cous Cous.

DINNER TIME

DO THE SALSA WITH A SALMON

The history of Salsa sauce originated with the Inca people. Salsa (combination of chilies, tomatoes and other spices) can be traced to the Aztecs, Mayans and Incas. The Spaniards first encountered tomatoes after their conquest of Mexico in 1519-1521, which marked the beginning of the history of Salsa sauce. Aztec lords combined tomatoes with chili peppers, ground squash seeds and consumed them mainly as a condiment served on turkey, venison, lobster, and fish. This combination was subsequently called salsa by Alonso de Molina in 1571.

INGREDIENTS

Salmon fillet
Small Roma Tomato, chopped
¼ Avocado, chopped
Clove of Garlic, crushed
Olive Oil
¼ Frozen Corn Kernels, cooked
¼ small Red Onion, chopped
2 ounce Cilantro, chopped

DIRECTIONS

Preheat oven.

Combine all ingredients, except Salmon, in a small bowl and refrigerate for 30 minutes.

Place Salmon of Cooking Tray and bake for 20 minutes.

Serve Salmon surrounded by the Salsa.

STOP THE SALT

NOT PEACHES & HERB...SALMON & HERBS!

Herbs have a variety of uses including culinary, medicinal, and in some cases spiritual usage. General usage of the term "herb" differs between culinary herbs and medicinal herbs. In medicinal or spiritual use any of the parts of the plant might be considered "herbs", including leaves, roots, flowers, seeds, resin, root bark, inner bark (and cambium), berries and sometimes the pericarp or other portions of the plant. In American botanical English the term "herb" is also used as an abbreviation of "herbaceous plant". This usage is rarely found in British English.

INGREDIENTS

Salmon Fillet
½ cup Low Sodium Breadcrumbs
1 tablespoon Chives
1 tablespoon Parsley
¼ tablespoon Garlic Powder
⅛ cup of Lemon Juice

DIRECTIONS

Preheat oven.

Place Salmon skin side down on baking sheet covered with Aluminum Foil.

Mix remaining ingredients together, except for the Lemon Juice.

Sprinkle Salmon with Lemon Juice and put Breadcrumb mixture on top of the fillet.

Spray lightly with Olive Oil Cooking Spray.

Serve with Broccoli and Barley.

DINNER TIME

THAT CHICK IS BROWN SUGAR

In the late 1800s, the newly consolidated refined white sugar industry, which did not have full control over brown sugar production, mounted a smear campaign against brown sugar, reproducing microscopic photographs of harmless but repulsive-looking microbes living in brown sugar. The effort was so successful that by 1900, a best-selling cookbook warned that brown sugar was of inferior quality and was susceptible to infestation by "a minute insect." But now, we know that is all wrong.

INGREDIENTS

Boneless, Skinless Chicken Breast
2 tablespoons Brown Sugar
Clove of Garlic, chopped
1 tablespoon Non Salted Butter
Black Pepper

DIRECTIONS

Set stove on Medium and melt butter in a Frying Pan.

Brown the Garlic in the Butter.

Add Chicken then add Pepper. Cook for 15-20 minutes until done.

When chicken is fully cooked add Brown Sugar.

Allow Sugar to melt. (Around 5 minutes.)

Serve with Brussels Sprouts and Ruby Red Potatoes.

STOP THE SALT

CASA ROLLIE (HOUSE OF SOMETHING)

In 1866, Elmire Jolicoeur, a French Canadian immigrant, invented the precursor of the modern casserole in Berlin, New Hampshire. The casseroles we know today are a relatively modern invention. Early casserole recipes consisted of rice that was pounded, pressed, and filled with a savory mixture of meats such as chicken or sweetbreads. Around the 1870s this sense of casserole seems to have slipped into its current sense. Cooking in earthenware containers has always been common in most nations, but the idea of casserole cooking as a one-dish meal became popular in America in the twentieth century, especially in the 1950s.

INGREDIENTS

Boneless Skinless Chicken Breast, cooked and cut into small pieces
¼ Broccoli Spears
½ can Low-Sodium Cream of Mushroom Soup
1 tablespoon Fat Free Mayo
½ Cup Reduced Fat Swiss Cheese, shredded

DIRECTIONS

Preheat oven.

In a small Casserole dish, mix Mayo and Soup.

Add Broccoli and Chicken and mix well.

Sprinkle with cheese.

Bake for 15 minutes or until Cheese melts.

DINNER TIME

I GOT YOUR FLOUNDA!

In its life cycle, an adult flounder has two eyes situated on one side of its head, while at hatching one eye is located on each side of its brain. One eye migrates to the other side of the body as a process of metamorphosis as it grows from larval to juvenile stage. As an adult, a flounder changes its habits and camouflages itself by lying on the bottom of the ocean floor as protection against predators. As a result, the eyes are then on the side which faces up. The side to which the eyes migrate is dependent on the species type.

INGREDIENTS

Flounder
¼ cup Mushrooms, chopped
⅓ cup Low Sodium or Panko Bread Crumbs
1 tablespoon Lemon Juice
1 teaspoon Low Sodium Soy Sauce
Black Pepper

DIRECTIONS

Preheat Oven

Place Flounder on Baking Dish.

Top with Bread Crumbs and Mushrooms.

Sprinkle with Pepper, Lemon Juice and Soy Sauce.

Bake.

Serve with Brown/White Rice mixture and Broccoli.

FISHY YOGURT
(DON'T WORRY IT'S NOT A NEW FLAVOR.)

The origins of yogurt are unknown. Analysis indicates that the bacteria may have originated on the surface of a plant. Milk may have become spontaneously and unintentionally infected through contact with plants, or bacteria may have been transferred via the udder of domestic milk-producing animals. The oldest writings mentioning yogurt have been attributed to Pliny the Elder, who remarked that certain "barbarous nations" knew how "to thicken the milk into a substance with an agreeable acidity."

INGREDIENTS

1 Swai Fillet
1½ tablespoons Low Fat Plain Yogurt
3 tablespoons Red Onion, chopped
1 teaspoon Chili Powder
1 teaspoon Lime juice

DIRECTIONS

Preheat oven.

Mix together Yogurt, Red Onion, Chili Powder and Lime juice.

Place Swai on cooking pan.

Top with mixture and put in the oven.

Serve with Green Peppers and Cous Cous.

WHITE, HE'S CORNY AND FLAKY

This idea for corn flakes began by accident when Dr. John Harvey Kellogg and his younger brother, Will Keith Kellogg, left some cooked wheat to sit while they attended to some pressing matters at the sanitarium they worked at. When they returned, they found that the wheat had gone stale, but being on a strict budget, they decided to continue to process it by forcing it through rollers, hoping to obtain long sheets of the dough. To their surprise, what they found instead were flakes, which they toasted and served to their patients.

INGREDIENTS

Whiting fillet
1 cup of Corn Flakes, crushed
1½ tablespoons Low Fat Mayo
1 teaspoon Dill
Dash of Cayenne Pepper

DIRECTIONS

Preheat oven.

Spray cooking pan with Non-Stick Olive Oil Spray.

Combine Corn Flakes, Dill and Cayenne Pepper in a bowl.

Brush Whiting on both sides with Mayo.

Press the Whiting in Corn Flake mixture until coated. Shake off excess.

Bake.

Remove from oven and serve with Ruby Red Potatoes and Green Beans.

CITRUS SALMON JUICE PACK

The first aluminum foil rolling plant, "Dr. Lauber, Neher & Cie." was opened in Emmishofen, Switzerland in 1910. The plant, owned by J.G. Neher & Sons, the aluminum manufacturers, started in 1886 in Schaffhausen, Switzerland, at the foot of the Rhine Falls, capturing the Falls energy to produce aluminum. Neher's sons, together with Dr. Lauber, discovered the endless rolling process and the use of aluminum foil as a protective barrier in December 1907. The first use of foil in the United States was in 1913 for wrapping Life Savers, candy bars, and gum.[1] Processes evolved over time to include the use of print, color, lacquer, laminate and the embossing of the aluminum.

INGREDIENTS

Salmon Fillet
1 cup Spinach
¼ small Yellow Onion, sliced
¼ cup Orange sliced with Juice
Black Pepper

DIRECTIONS

Preheat oven. Put a good amount of foil on a Cooking Pan and coat with Nonstick Cooking Spray.

Place Salmon in center of foil.

Top the Salmon with a dash of Black Pepper, Spinach, Onion and Oranges with Juice.

Wrap up foil to make a closed packet.

Bake and serve with Brown Rice.

CHICKEN MARS ALA JUPITER

Chicken Marsala's name originates from the particular wine, Marsala, used to create the sauce. Marsala is produced in Sicily, Italy, and is one of the country's most famous wines. Its flavor can range from sweet to dry, and it is used as a dessert wine or aperitif. The popularity of the Chicken dish dates back to the 19th century, when it most likely originated with English families who lived in the western Sicily region, where the Marsala wine is produced.

INGREDIENTS

Boneless, Skinless Chicken Breast
1/16 Cup of Flour
Olive Oil
1/4 tablespoon Butter
2 ounces Mushrooms, sliced
1½ ounces Marsala Wine
Ground Black Pepper
Dash of Oregano
Dash of Garlic powder

DIRECTIONS

In a bowl, stir together Flour, Garlic, Pepper and Oregano.

Dredge Chicken in mixture to lightly coat.

Heat the Olive Oil and Butter in a skillet over medium heat.

Fry Chicken for 3 minutes until lightly browned.

Turn chicken over and add Mushrooms. Cook for 3 more minutes.

Pour Marsala wine over Chicken. Reduce heat to low and simmer for 15 more minutes.

Serve with Broccoli.

BAKED CHICK-ON

Onions can make a person cry. Eye irritation can be avoided by cutting onions under running water or submerged in a basin of water. Leaving the root end intact also reduces irritation as the onion base has a higher concentration of sulfur compounds than the rest of the bulb. Refrigerating the onions before use reduces the enzyme reaction rate and using a fan can blow the gas away from the eyes. The more often one chops up onions, the less one experiences eye irritation

INGREDIENTS

Skinless, Boneless Chicken Breast
½ medium Onion, sliced into rings
4 Garlic cloves, sliced thinly
2 tablespoons White Wine
1 tablespoon Lemon Juice
Paprika to taste

DIRECTIONS

Preheat oven to 350.

Lightly spray Baking Dish with Non-Stick Olive Oil spray.

Layer bottom of Baking Dish with ½ the Onions and ½ the Garlic.

Pour the Lemon Juice and White Wine in the Baking Dish.

Place Chicken in the dish and season with Paprika.

Top with the remaining Onions and Garlic.

Bake for 25 minutes.

SPICY STEWEY SNAP SNAP

Stewed tomatoes are tomatoes that have been peeled and cooked just long enough to soften their flesh and release their flavors. The fruits keep their shape throughout this process, but become aromatic and are often added to pasta sauces or other dishes requiring tomatoes. Many cooks stew excess tomatoes as a way to preserve them for later use.

INGREDIENTS

Red Snapper fillet
6 ounces No Salt Added Stewed Tomatoes
2 tablespoons White Wine
Olive Oil
¼ onion, chopped
½ Garlic Clove, crushed
¼ teaspoon crushed Red Pepper flakes
Black Pepper to taste

DIRECTIONS

In a skillet heat Olive Oil on medium.

Add Onion, Garlic and Red Pepper. Saute' until the onion is soft.

Add the Tomatoes with juice and White wine. Reduce heat to low and simmer.

Break up tomatoes with spoon as sauce cooks.

Once the sauce starts to thicken add Snapper and push them down in pan.

Cover and cook for 15-20 minutes until fish flakes.

Serve over White Rice.

JUST FOR THE HALIBUT

Halibut is a flatfish, from the family of the right-eye flounders. Other flatfish are also called halibut. The name is derived from haly (holy) and butt (flat fish), for its popularity on Catholic holy days. Halibut are demersal fish which live in the North Pacific and the North Atlantic oceans. At birth, they have an eye on each side of the head, and swim like a salmon. After six months, one eye migrates to the other side, making them look more like flounder. At the same time, the stationary-eyed side darkens to match the top side, while the other side remains white. This color scheme disguises halibut from above and from below and is known as countershading.

INGREDIENTS

Halibut fillet
½ Celery stalk, cleaned and chopped
¼ Green Bell Pepper, seeded and chopped
¼ Yellow Onion, thinly sliced
1 Garlic clove, crushed
6 ounces No Salt Added Diced Tomatoes
2 tablespoons Olive Oil
3 tablespoons Parsley
Black Pepper to taste

DIRECTIONS

Preheat oven.

Place Halibut in a Baking Pan.

Sprinkle with Pepper.

Stir Oil, Parsley, Onion, Celery, Bell Pepper, Tomatoes and Garlic together.

Pour over Halibut.

Bake and serve with Brown Rice.

SAUCED PORK

The center cut or pork loin chop includes a large T shaped bone, and is structurally similar to the beef T-bone steak. Rib chops come from the rib portion of the loin, and are similar to rib eye steaks. Blade or shoulder chops come from the spine, and tend to contain large amounts of connective tissue. The sirloin chop is taken from the (rear) leg end and also contains a large amount of connective tissue. The so-called "Iowa Chop" is a thick center cut; the term was coined in 1976 by the Iowa Pork Producers Association. A "Bacon Chop" is cut from the shoulder end and leaves the pork belly meat attached.

INGREDIENTS

Pork Chop
¼ Yellow Onion, chopped
¼ Green Bell Pepper, seeded and chopped
4 ounces No Salt Added or Low Sodium Tomato Sauce
Garlic Powder to taste
Black Pepper to taste
Olive Oil
Flour

DIRECTIONS

In a skillet heat Olive Oil on medium.

Dredge Pork Chop in flour and add to pan. Cook until nicely browned on both sides.

Remove Pork Chop and add Onion and Bell Pepper and cook and stir for 5 minutes.

Return Pork Chop to skillet and pour in Tomato Sauce.

Allow sauce to bubble and then reduce heat to low.

Simmer for 30 minutes and season with Garlic Powder and Black Pepper.

Serve with a side of Cous Cous.

PARM E. SAN, ITALIAN CHICKEN ESQUIRE

The dish is claimed by both Campania and Sicily. While "parmigiana" usually means "from Parma" (in Northern Italy), the dish is not part of the cuisine of Parma. It is a Southern Italian dish. Parmigiana is also used in the names of unrelated dishes that do form part of the cuisine of Parma, such as trippa alla parmigiana (Parma-style tripe). In Argentina it is called "Milanesa" (if beef or veal), "de Pollo" (chicken), "de Berenjena" (eggplant) or "de Cerdo" (pork) ending in "a la Napolitana" when served with a slice of ham and topped with a variety of melted cheeses and tomato sauce and/or a slice of tomato; or simply Milanesa if served without toppings and garnished with a slice of lemon.

INGREDIENTS

Boneless, Skinless Chicken breast
2 tablespoons Low Sodium or Panko Bread Crumbs
1 Egg, beaten
6 ounces No Salt Added Pasta Sauce
1 slice Low Fat Provolone
Spaghetti, cooked

DIRECTIONS

Preheat oven.

Dip Chicken in Egg and then coat both sides with Bread Crumbs.

Spray Baking Sheet with non-stick Olive Oil Cooking Spray.

Place Chicken on sheet and bake 20 minutes, flipping halfway.

Take Chicken out and switch oven to Broil.

Pour Sauce over Chicken, top with Cheese and broil for 2 minutes until cheese melts.

Serve over Spaghetti.

DINNER TIME

MU MU HON CHICKEN

There are many types of honey mustard, because there are many types of both honey and mustard. The French have created their own gentle version, but countries with sharper mustards also combine them with honey. British mustard is quite sharp and strong, and is used quite sparingly on its own. When combined with honey, the Brits use it on everything from lamb to vegetables. Other cultures have recently adapted honey mustard to their own ingredients. Many Japanese restaurants use a honey-mustard dressing on various vegetables and salads, and some Chinese restaurants use it as a change-up on the traditional Chinese chicken salad. It has even found a home in Korea, where it is used with noodles and vegetables.

INGREDIENTS

Boneless Skinless Chicken Breast
2½ tablespoons Honey
2½ tablespoons Mustard
Dash of Dried Basil
Dash of Paprika
Dash of dried Parsley

DIRECTIONS

Preheat Oven.

In a small bowl, combine the honey, mustard, paprika, basil and parsley. Mix well.

Spray cooking pan and place chicken on it.

Spoon ½ the mixture on chicken and brush to cover.

Cook for 10 minutes, then turn and cover with the other ½ of the mixture.

Let cool for 5 minutes.

Serve with rice and asparagus.

CHOKE N' CHICKEN

Believe it or not there was once an "Artichoke War of 1935." Ciro "The Artichoke King" Terranova was a New York City gangster and one time underboss of the Morello crime family. Ciro earned his nickname, "the Artichoke King", by purchasing artichokes at $6.00 a crate from California, then selling them in New York at a 30-40% profit. Ciro's violent reputation preceded him, frightening vegetable sellers into buying them. Even the fields back in California were hacked down in the middle of the night to scare bring fear to those farmers and distributors that didn't co-operate. Taking action these "artichoke wars" led Fiorello La Guardia one of New York's famous Mayors (whom they named the airport after) to appear at The Bronx Terminal Market and to institute a city-wide ban on the sale, display, and possession of artichokes.

INGREDIENTS

Boneless Skinless Chicken Breast
3 ounces of canned Chopped Artichoke Hearts, drained
2 tablespoons low fat Mayonnaise
2 tablespoons grated Parmesan Cheese
Pinch of Garlic Powder

DIRECTIONS

Preheat Oven.

In a small bowl, mix together all ingredients except the Chicken.

Place Chicken of sprayed cooking pan.

Cover evenly with Artichoke mixture.

Bake uncovered for 20 minutes.

Serve with Quinoa and sliced Roma Tomatoes.

SAL POTION #1

Salmon migrate up to 4,000 miles from the ocean to freshwater areas to spawn (or lay eggs). They also must swim against very strong ocean currents just to reach freshwater, and then swim upstream against the powerful flow of the river. Additionally, they must leap clear of the water to get above falls, and do all this while avoiding predators–who know they are there and want to catch and eat them. They do all this only to die only minutes after spawning.

INGREDIENTS

Salmon fillet
3 ounces Low Sodium Chicken Broth
½ small Red Onion, quartered
⅓ pound Red Potatoes, halved
Black Pepper, dash
Olive Oil

DIRECTIONS

In a skillet, heat oil over medium-high.

Add onions and season with pepper.

Cook 4 minutes until golden brown, turning once.

Add potatoes and broth and bring to a boil.

Reduce to a simmer and cover.

Cook until potatoes are tender, about 20 minutes.

Place salmon on top of potatoes.

Cover and cook for 7 to 9 minutes.

Serve with the onions, potatoes and cooking liquid.

STOP THE SALT

YELLOW FISHROOM

Two cool Mushroom facts. Mushrooms have been used medicinally in China for more than 6,000 years. Ancient Chinese and Japanese practitioners have for centuries used specialty mushrooms but it is only now that scientists are learning how some mushrooms help the immune system and there are hieroglyphics from 4600 years ago featuring mushrooms. Mushrooms were declared to be a food for royalty and no ordinary citizens could touch them. It was also believed that whoever ate these mushrooms would become immortal.

INGREDIENTS

1 Striped-Bass Fillet
½ pound Cremini Mushrooms
Olive Oil
2 tablespoons parsley
Black Pepper
1 Squash, halved long ways

DIRECTIONS

Preheat Oven.

Toss Mushrooms and Squash with Olive Oil and Parsley.

Place on baking sheet and roast for 10 minutes or until lightly browned.

Rub fish with olive oil and add black pepper to taste.

Place Fish on top of Mushrooms and Squash and cook for 10 to 12 minutes.

Serve fish and mushrooms with roasted yellow squash.

THAT ROSIE CHICK

The word Rosemary is derived from the Latin words ros (dew) and marinus (sea). Rosemary is actually a bush perennial that grows in abundance in the Mediterranean area such as Spain, Italy, Portugal, Southern France, Greece and North Africa as well as in isolated areas of Turkey, Lebanon and Egypt. It is one of the most common aromatic wild plants of the Mediterranean landscape, especially in rocky limestone hillsides adjoining the seaside and was relocated to England by the Romans in the eighth century, primarily in the southern part of the country.

INGREDIENTS

2 large Chicken Thighs, bone-in, skin-on
Olive Oil
1½ teaspoons dried Rosemary
½ Lemon, sliced
Black Pepper, dash

DIRECTIONS

Place Chicken in dish and top with Rosemary, Lemon Slices and Black Pepper.

Drizzle with Olive Oil and then cover and refrigerate for 30 minutes.

Preheat Oven and set stove to medium high heat.

Place Chicken in pan, skin side down.

Cook Chicken for 5 minutes, flip it and cook for 5 minutes more.

Once both sides are brown put in a baking dish.

Bake for 15 minutes

Let rest for 5 minutes and serve with Zucchini and Cous Cous.

VAMPIRES NEED NOT APPLY STEAK

New York strip steak is a cut of beef that goes by many different names. It is also known as a Kansas City steak, a Delmonico steak and a strip loin. The steak known as New York strip comes from the cow's short loin, which is located on the upper back of the animal. The muscles here do little work and thus yield a tender cut of meat. In 1837, Delmonico's Restaurant opened in Manhattan. Self-proclaimed as "America's first fine dining restaurant," one of its signature dishes was a cut from the short loin that was called a Delmonico steak. Due to its association with the city, it has since been referred to as a New York strip.

INGREDIENTS

12 ounce New York Steak
½ Bulb Garlic, cloves separated and peeled
Black Pepper

DIRECTIONS

Preheat Broiler.

Cut garlic cloves into lengthwise strips.

Using a sharp knife, punch holes into the Steak.

Stuff garlic in holes and cover and refrigerate for four hours.

Place stuff steaks on a cooking pan garlic side up.

Broil for 6 minutes.

Turn and season with pepper. Cook for four more minutes.

Serve with Corn on the Cob and Baked Potato.

DINNER TIME

GOOMBAH CODDY

What's the difference between a black and green olive? The color of the olive corresponds to the ripeness of the fruit when picked. That's it. Green olives are picked before ripening, and black olives are picked while ripe. And because raw olives are mostly inedible, both varieties normally undergo some form of curing process, either by being packed in salt, brined, pickled, or soaked in oil (or even just water) before being eaten. Generally, green olives are denser, firmer and bitterer than black olives. The taste and texture of any olive, however, ultimately depend on the method and duration of curation.

INGREDIENTS

Cod fillet
½ Onion, thinly sliced
½ 14.5 ounce can of low sodium diced tomatoes
1 clove garlic, minced
12 low sodium large, canned Black Olives, sliced
¼ cup White Wine
1 teaspoon parsley
Olive Oil

DIRECTIONS

Add Olive Oil to a large frying pan. Saute onions and garlic for 5 minutes on medium until softened.

Stir in Tomatoes, Olives, Parsley and Wine and simmer for 5 minutes.

Place Cod in sauce. Cover and cook for 10 minutes.

Serve over White Rice.

STOP THE SALT

SALMO DIJIO

Dijon mustard originated in 1856, when Jean Naigeon of Dijon substituted verjuice, the acidic "green" juice of unripe grapes, for vinegar in the traditional mustard recipe. Most mustard from Dijon today contains white wine rather than verjuice. "Dijon mustard" is not a protected food name. While there remain mustard factories in Dijon and adjoining towns, most mustard described as "Dijon" is manufactured elsewhere. Even that produced in France is made almost exclusively from Canadian mustard seed.

INGREDIENTS

Salmon Fillet
2 tablespoons unsalted butter, melted
1½ tablespoons Dijon Mustard
2¼ teaspoons honey
2 tablespoons low sodium Bread Crumbs
2 tablespoons Pecans, finely chopped
Black Pepper
2 teaspoons Parsley

DIRECTIONS

Preheat oven

Spray cooking pan with non-stick cooking spray.

In a small bowl, stir together butter, mustard and honey.

In another small bowl, mix together bread crumbs, pecans and parsley.

Brush Salmon with honey mustard mixture and sprinkle the salmon with bread crumbs mix.

Cook for 15-20 minutes.

Serve with Green Beans and Barley.

SAMMIES & SUCH

STOP THE SALT

TUNA SALAD CACTUS TORTILLA TACO AND HOLDING COMPANY

Say that title five times real quick. Nopal Cactus is referred to in English as Prickly Pear and is a main ingredient in Cactus Tortillas. The nutritious components of Nopal have curative and preventive properties. It reduces cholesterol and it helps in the assimilation of nutrients to regulate the levels of glucose in the blood. It also reduces plaque formation in the veins and arteries improving circulation. The calcium present helps prevent osteoporosis and its high content of fiber helps improve the entire digestive system. All of this combines to help improve the blood and that helps diuresis as an aid in cleansing the kidneys.

INGREDIENTS

Can of Low Sodium Tuna Fish
¼ Red Onion
¼ Cucumber
¼ Avocado
1 tablespoon Low Fat Mayo
Cayenne Pepper
Black Pepper
½ Lime
3 Cactus Tortillas – 4 inch

DIRECTIONS

Drain Tuna Fish and place in small bowl. Add Mayo, Cayenne Pepper and Black Pepper. Squeeze in juice from Lime and mix all ingredients together.

Chop Red Onion into small pieces. Then slice Cucumber into thin slices and avocado into four length wise pieces.

Place Tortillas on plate and add Tuna to each one. Top with Onion and lie Cucumber and Avocado down.

Roll up like a Soft Taco and enjoy with a Side Salad.

CHICKY CHICKY CHUNKS

Just because Chicken Strips, Chicken Nuggets and Chicken Fingers are worn out. A chicken breast is composed of two separate muscles: a large one and a tapered narrow flap In order to fabricate a chicken breast that is tidy, trim, and at an even thickness so that it cooks at the same rate, the two fillets must be separated. Given that most Americans prefer to have pieces of protein on their plates that are large enough to cut, the larger ones are more for dinner. But what of the smaller fillets, commonly known as "tenders"? The answer for chicken producers was to sell them as finger food. We will conquer both worlds with this dish.

INGREDIENTS

Boneless Skinless Chicken Breast
Olive Oil Cooking Spray
¼ cup Panko or Low Sodium Bread Crumbs
Crushed Red Pepper
Black Pepper

DIRECTIONS

Preheat Oven.

Cut Chicken into around 8 smaller pieces.

Mix Bread Crumbs, Black Pepper and Red Pepper and put in Quart-Sized Ziploc.

Spray each Chicken piece with Oil Oil.

Place in bag and shake until coated.

Put on Cooking Pan and bake for 20-25 minutes. (Depending on desired crispness.)

Plate and serve with Corn on the Cob and Baby Red Potatoes.

STOP THE SALT

SASSY SARDINE BOAT

This dish is a dish. Very attractive and would most definitely win the Swim Suit Contest in a Beauty Pageant. The term sardine was first used in English during the early 15th century and may come from the Mediterranean island of Sardinia, around which sardines were once abundant. Also, Females will grow faster than males and some individuals mature in their first year, most in their second. Maximum age 13-25 years, most are less than 8 years.

INGREDIENTS

One 4¼ ounce can of Low Sodium Sardines
1 tablespoon Low Fat Mayonnaise
Small piece of Red Onion
Black Pepper
½ Lemon
Medium Avocado

DIRECTIONS

Open can and drain fluid from Sardines. Put Fish in bowl and mash with a fork.

Chop Red Onion and add to Fish along with Mayonnaise. Mix up.

Add some Black Pepper to taste and squeeze juice from the Lemon. Mix again.

Cut Avocado in half and remove pit.

Place Avocado halves on plate and spoon Sardine mixture into them.

Serve with a Side Salad.

HUH? A SANDWICH CALLED BLAT?

Actually BLAT is short for a Bacon, Lettuce, Avocado and Tomato Sandwich. The traditional BLT evolved from the tea sandwiches served before 1900 at a similar time to the club sandwich, although it is unclear when the name BLT became the norm. In 1963, pop art sculptor Claes Oldenburg created a giant BLT sandwich sculpture, currently on display at the Whitney Museum of American Art. It measures 32 by 39 inches (81 cm × 99 cm) and uses vinyl, kapok and wood, painted in acrylic. Every time it is moved, it must be restacked, which means it varies between exhibits.

INGREDIENTS

2 strips Low Sodium or Turkey Bacon
Low Sodium Grain or Wheat Bread
2 slices of Tomato
Romaine Lettuce
¼ Avocado
1 tablespoon Low Fat Mayonnaise

DIRECTIONS

Place Bacon strips on a Microwave safe small plate lined with some Paper Towel. Cook on high for 2 – 4 minutes. (Microwave power will vary.)

Toast Bread.

Separate Avocado from skin and cut into thin slices.

Brush Mayo on top piece of Toast.

Place Tomato, then Lettuce, then Bacon, then Avocado on lower piece of Toast and cut sandwich in half.

Serve with Kale Chips.

VEGGIEMITE SANDWICH

A Vegemite sandwich became a popular term from the song "Down Under" by the Aussie group Men at Work. However, Vegemite doesn't really sound too tasty. It's a dark brown Australian food paste made from brewers' yeast extract, a by-product of beer manufacturing, various vegetables and wheat and spice additives. It is salty, slightly bitter and malty and is a spread for sandwiches, toast, crumpets and cracker biscuits as well as a filling for pastries. Doesn't sound good, but this sandwich is.

INGREDIENTS

½ Zucchini, cut diagonally into ½ inch slices
½ Red Bell Pepper, cut into quarters
½ small Onion cut into quarters
Olive Oil
Black Pepper
2 pieces Whole Grain Bread
1 leave of Romaine Lettuce, trimmed
2 slices of Tomato
1 tablespoon Mayonnaise

DIRECTIONS

Preheat oven.

Mix Zucchini, Red Pepper and Onion together. Add Olive Oil and Black Pepper and coat Vegetables.

Put a good amount of foil on a Cooking Pan and coat with Nonstick Cooking Spray.

Roast Vegetables for 30 – 45 minutes until golden brown, turning once during cooking process.

Remove from oven and let cool.

Put mayonnaise on one slice of bread. On other place Veggies topped with Romaine and Tomato. Assemble sandwich and cut in half.

Serve with a Side Salad.

SORT OF DEEP DISH PIZZA

The Eggplant is related to both the tomato and the potato and this fruit is botanically classified as a berry. It is also known as the aubergine, brinjal, melongene, or guinea squash. Some 18th-century European versions were yellow or white and resembled goose or hen's eggs, hence the name eggplant. The plant is native to the Indian Subcontinent. It has been cultivated in southern and eastern Asia since prehistory. The first known written record of the plant is found in Qí mín yào shù, an ancient Chinese agricultural treatise completed in 544. But today it's going to be the crust for a popular dish.

INGREDIENTS

¼ to ½ of an Eggplant, cut into ½ inch round pieces
¼ cup Low Sodium Pasta Sauce
½ cup Low Fat Shredded Parmesan Cheese
Olive Oil
Black Pepper

DIRECTIONS

Preheat oven.

Put a good amount of foil on a Cooking Pan and coat with Nonstick Cooking Spray.

Brush both sides of Eggplant with Olive Oil and season with pepper.

Place on pan and cook for 6-8 minutes until tender, turning once.

Spread Pasta Sauce on each one.

Top with Shredded Cheese.

Cook 3 – 5 minutes until Cheese is melted.

STOP THE SALT

TURKEY FLORENTINE: MAN OF THE STREETS

"A la Florentine" means in the style of Florence, and usually refers to dishes which contain spinach (and frequently together with Mornay sauce), especially eggs, fish and white meat. The connection to Florence, Italy is a little obscure, but there is a story that Catherine de Medici introduced spinach to the Court of France (or at least made it popular). To honor her Italian roots, she supposedly dubbed any dish containing spinach "Florentine". This dish not only had spinach in it, but is served on it. Pretty snazzy!

INGREDIENTS

Ground Turkey
1¼ cups of bagged Spinach
2 tablespoons Low Sodium Bread Crumbs
2 tablespoons Egg Substitute
Clove of Garlic, crushed
Ground Black Pepper
1 tablespoon Grated Parmesan Cheese
Olive Oil

DIRECTIONS

Chop ¼ cup of Spinach coarsely and put into Mixing Bowl.

Add Ground Turkey, Bread Crumbs, Egg Substitute, Garlic, Cheese and Black Pepper.

Shape into a Patty.

Coat Frying Pan with Olive Oil.

Over medium heat, brown Burger on each side.

Turn down temperature to low, cover pan and cook until all the pink in the middle is gone.

Serve on top of the remaining Spinach, cooked.

PUT THE LIME IN THE CHICKEN...THEN IN A TORTILLA

According to Mayan legend, tortillas were invented by a peasant for his hungry king in ancient times. The first tortillas discovered, which date back to approximately 10,000 BC, were made of native maize with dried kernel. The Aztecs used a lot of maize, both eaten straight from the cob and in recipes. They ground the maize, and used the cornmeal to make dough called masa. This bread made from maize was later given the name tortilla (little cake) by the Spanish.

INGREDIENTS

1 Chicken Breast
¼ Onion, sliced
½ Green Pepper, seeded and sliced
1 tablespoon Lime Juice
1 tablespoon Olive Oil
½ tablespoon Crushed Red Pepper
½ tablespoon Black Pepper
Corn Tortillas

DIRECTIONS

Combine Olive Oil, Crushed Red and Black Pepper and Lime Juice in a container. Add Chicken. Cover and marinate in refrigerator for 15-30 minutes.

Add new Olive Oil to pan and heat on medium.

Remove Chicken from container and it and the vegetables to the pan.

Cover and cook for 15 minutes.

Remove and cut Chicken into slices.

Heat the Tortilla in a Microwave for 1 minute.

Top the Tortilla off with the Chicken and Vegetables.

Wrap it all up.

Serve with Brown Rice and Low Sodium Black Beans.

FORGOT THIS SHRIMP DISH

In the great movie, Forrest Gump, Bubba lists 21 kinds of shrimp if you include the cooking methods. As quoted directly from the movie, "Shrimp is the fruit of the sea. You can barbecue it, boil it, broil it, bake it, sauté it. There's, um, shrimp kabobs, shrimp creole, shrimp gumbo, pan fried, deep fried, stir fried. There's pineapple shrimp and lemon shrimp, coconut shrimp, pepper shrimp, shrimp soup, shrimp stew, shrimp salad, shrimp in potatoes, shrimp burger, shrimp sandwich. That's, that's about it." However, he forgot this great dish. The Shrimp BLT!

INGREDIENTS

6-8 deveined Shrimp depending on size
2 strips Low Sodium or Turkey Bacon
Low Sodium Grain or Wheat Bread
2 slices of Tomato
Romaine Lettuce
1 tablespoon Low Fat Mayonnaise

DIRECTIONS

Boil water in a small pot. Add Shrimp and cook for 3-5 minutes. Let cool and peel after.

Place Bacon strips on a Microwave safe small plate lined with some Paper Towel. Cook on high for 2 – 4 minutes. (Microwave power will vary.)

Toast Bread.

Brush Mayo on top piece of Toast.

Place Tomato, then Lettuce, then Bacon, then Shrimp on lower piece of Toast and cut sandwich in half.

Serve with a Side Salad.

YES, PATTY SALMON CAN!

The "father of canning" is the Frenchman Nicolas Appert. In 1795, he began experimenting with ways to preserve foodstuffs, placing food in sealed glass jars and then placing the jars in boiling water. During the first years of the Napoleonic Wars, the French government offered a 12,000-franc prize to anyone who could devise a cheap and effective method of preserving large amounts of food. Appert submitted his invention and won the prize in January 1810. So we can thank him for this recipe.

INGREDIENTS

½ can Low Sodium Salmon (6 ounces)
¼ medium Onion, finely chopped
½ small stalk of Celery, finely chopped
2 tablespoons Egg Substitute
¼ cup Low Sodium Bread Crumbs
¼ teaspoon Chili Powder
Olive Oil

DIRECTIONS

Heat Olive Oil on medium in a frying pan.

Combine all other ingredients in a bowl and shape into a Burger Patty.

Heat each side for 5 minutes or until browned.

Serve with Spinach and Cous Cous.

STOP THE SALT

TUNA I MELT WITH YOU

"I Melt With You" was a great 80's song by the band Modern English. A melt sandwich (also known in Australia, New Zealand, and the United Kingdom as a toasted cheese sandwich or toastie) is a type of sandwich consisting of bread, some sort of filling, and a layer of cheese, sometimes grated. The sandwich is then grilled or fried until the cheese is melted. It may be served as an open face sandwich or a closed face one. Don't get the song and sandwich confused. (Not that anyone could.)

INGREDIENTS

6 ounce can of No Salt Added Tuna, drained
1 tablespoon Low Fat Mayonnaise
Celery to liking, chopped finely
Onion to liking, chopped finely
2 slices Low Fat Swiss Cheese
2 slices of Tomato
2 pieces of Grain or Whole Wheat Bread
Black Pepper

DIRECTIONS

Mix Tuna, Mayo, Celery, Onion and Pepper in bowl.

Lightly toast Bread.

Put bread on a microwave safe plate. Top with Tuna, then Tomato and then Cheese.

Microwave on high for 5 minutes or until Cheese is melted.

Serve with your favorite side.

PHILLY SUBURB CHEESESTEAK

Philadelphians Pat and Harry Olivieri are often credited with inventing the cheesesteak sandwich by serving chopped steak on hoagie rolls in the early 1930s. They began selling this variation of steak sandwiches at their hot dog stand near south Philadelphia's Italian Market. They became so popular that Pat opened up his own restaurant which still operates today as Pat's King of Steaks. The sandwich was originally prepared without cheese; Olivieri claims provolone cheese was first added by Joe "Cocky Joe" Lorenza, a manager at the Ridge Avenue location.

INGREDIENTS

2 Minute Steaks
1½ slices of Low Fat Swiss Cheese
⅛ White Onion, chopped
Handful of Mushrooms, sliced
2 slices of Whole Grain bread
Olive Oil

DIRECTIONS

Add Olive Oil to small pan and heat on Medium.

Add Onion and Mushroom and cook for 7-10 minutes until tender. Remove from heat.

Place Minute Steak in dry pan. Cook until it appears wet and flip. Repeat with other steak.

Place two steaks on microwave safe plate, lined with a Paper Towel.

Top with Onion, Mushroom and Cheese. Microwave on medium, 1-2 minutes until cheese melts.

Serve on bread with one of your favorite sides.

T.O. STADAS

Tostada is a Spanish word meaning "toasted". In Latin America it is the name of different local dishes which are toasted or use a toasted ingredient as the main base of their preparation. Even though the tortilla is fried; the meaning sticks with it. In Mexican usage, tostada usually refers to a flat or bowl-shaped (like a bread bowl) tortilla that is deep fried. It may also refer to any dish using a tostada as a base. It can be consumed alone, or used a base for other foods. Corn tortillas are usually used for tostadas, although tostadas made of wheat flour may occasionally be found.

INGREDIENTS

Small boneless Chicken Breast
2 6-inch Corn Tortillas
½ Poblano Pepper, seeded and chopped
¼ cup Frozen Corn, cooked
½ cup grape tomatoes, quartered
½ of Lime, juiced
½ tablespoon Chili Powder
2 ounces Low Fat Mexican Cheese
¼ Avocado, diced
1 tablespoon Cilantro

DIRECTIONS

Preheat Oven to 350.

Add Olive Oil to small frying pan. Add Chicken and cover. Cook for 15 minutes, turning once.

Do the same in another frying pan and add chopped Peppers. Cook until the outside start to char.

Spray one side of each Tortilla with Non-Stick Olive Oil Cooking Spray.

Bake until crisp around 10 minutes, flipping once.

In a bowl mix cooked Peppers, Corn, Tomatoes, Lime Juice and Chili Powder.

Divide mixture on top of the Tortillas. Add Chicken and Cheese and cook until cheese melts.

Remove from oven and top with Avocado and Cilantro.

SAMMY AVOCADO, MALE PROSTITUTE

It is believed that the avocado, originated in the state of Puebla, Mexico. The native, undomesticated variety is known as a criollo, and is small, with dark black skin, and contains a large seed. The oldest evidence of avocado use was found in a cave located in Coxcatlán, Puebla, Mexico, that dates to around 10,000 BC. The avocado tree also has a long history of cultivation in Central and South America; a water jar shaped like an avocado, dating to AD 900, was discovered in the pre-Incan city of Chan Chan.

INGREDIENTS

1 small Avocado, skinned and cut into thin slices
2 Tomato slices
Small handful of Sprouts
Whole Wheat slim
1 tablespoon Low Fat Mayo
Black Pepper

DIRECTIONS

Brush one side of slim with Mayo.

Place Tomato slices on bottom of slim.

Top with Avocado and then Sprouts.

Sprinkle Black Pepper to taste.

Serve with favorite side.

TOMMY AND SAMMY SITTING IN A TREE

A tomato is the edible, often red fruit from the plant Solanum lycopersicum, commonly known as a tomato plant. Both the species and its use as a food originated in Mexico, and spread around the world following the Spanish colonization of the Americas. While it is botanically a fruit, it is considered a vegetable for culinary purposes, which has caused some confusion. The tomato belongs to the nightshade family.

INGREDIENTS

4 slices Tomato
¼ cup Spinach
2 pieces of Whole Wheat or 8 Grain bread
2 tablespoons Reduced Fat Mayo
1 Garlic Clove, crushed
Black Pepper, a dash
Dried Basil, a dash

DIRECTIONS

Lightly toast bread.

Mix Mayo, Garlic, Black Pepper and Basil.

Spread mixture on top piece of toast.

Layer bottom piece of toast with Spinach then add Tomatoes.

Assemble sandwich and slice in half.

Serve with favorite side.

SAMMIES & SUCH

HOW ABOUT SOME BREAD WITH THESE VEGGIES

Vegetable sandwich is the most common type of sandwich in India. It is a purely vegetarian item (though not vegan if butter is used), and is often seen prepared and served fresh by roadside vendors as well as in many restaurants. Cheese may be added, if available, and the sandwich is usually open to customization by adding or withholding certain ingredients or leaving it untoasted. Innumerable variations are available changing from location and vendors, the unusual ones being Szechuan vegetable sandwich and Russian sandwich.

INGREDIENTS

2 slices Whole Wheat or 8 Grain Bread
1 slice of Low Fat Swiss Cheese
4 slices of Cucumber
1 layer of Spinach
3 rings of Green Bell Pepper
3 rings of sliced Red Onion
2 slices of Tomato
1 teaspoon Spicy Brown Mustard

DIRECTIONS

Lightly toast Bread.

Spread mustard on top piece of toast.

Place Spinach on bottom piece of toast.

Add Tomato, then Cucumber, followed by Red Onion then Green Pepper.

Top with slice of Swiss Cheese.

Assemble sandwich and slice in half.

Serve with favorite side.

STOP THE SALT

THIS AIN'T YOUR MOM'S TUNA SANDWICH

Tuna salad is an early twentieth century recipe. Why? Because canned tuna was first introduced and mass marketed to the American public in 1903. The Tuna Sandwich has been called "the mainstay of almost everyone's American childhood" and "the staple of the snatched office lunch for a generation". In the United States, 52% of canned tuna is used for sandwiches.

INGREDIENTS

Can of low sodium Tuna, drained
¼ Avocado, peeled and cubed
⅛ Red Onion, diced
1 teaspoon Lemon Juice
1 teaspoon Olive Oil
½ teaspoon Parsley
1 Whole Wheat Sandwich Slim

DIRECTIONS

Mix all ingredients except for the Slim.

Spoon Tuna Salad on Slim.

Serve with favorite side.

POOOOOR-TA-BELLA, POR-TA-BELLA, POR-TA-BELLA!

Portabellas are a large dark brown mushroom, which is simply a fully mature Cremini. They are 3-7 days older than Crimini mushrooms when harvested. The name portabella was popularized in the 1980s to sell a then unglamorous mushroom. Because it is harvested later, the portabella can easily reach 5 inches in diameter, and is packed with concentrated flavor. In the matter of portabella versus portobello, both spellings are used. However, the Mushroom Council has adopted the two "a" version to establish some consistency.

INGREDIENTS

1 Portabella Mushroom Cap, 3-4"
Slice of Low Fat Swiss
¼ Onion of choice
Whole Wheat Sandwich Slim
Olive Oil

DIRECTIONS

Preheat Broiler.

Brush Olive Oil on both sides of Portabella and set aside.

Add Olive Oil into a Frying Pan and heat on medium. Add onions and saute'.

Place Portabella on baking sheet and place and broil for 8 minutes.

Flip. Brush with more olive oil and cook for 6 more minutes.

Add onion and then Swiss and continue to cook for 2 more minutes or until cheese is melted.

Serve on Slim with favorite side.

STOP THE SALT

ALMOST EVERYTHING BAGEL BURGER

According to the New Yorker the Everything Bagel was created 30 years ago, when then teenager David Gussin was sweeping up burnt seed scraps at a Queens, New York bagel shop. He saved them in a bin, and voilà—another flukelike creation story. But was Gussin really first? According to Seth Godin, an author on marketing tactics and theories, he was already making them in 1977, not "around 1980," as Gussin claimed in the piece. Well, we will never know the truth so just enjoy this recipe.

INGREDIENTS

¼ pound Hamburger patty
2 ounces Cream Cheese
1 thick slice medium Tomato
1 slice large Red Onion
1 Everything Bagel Thin, lightly toasted
Olive Oil

DIRECTIONS

Heat frying pan over medium heat and add Olive Oil.

Grill Hamburger on one side for 4 minutes, flip, and repeat. (For a medium cooked burger.)

Place Hamburger on bottom of Bagel Thin and add Tomato and then Red Onion.

Spread Cream Cheese on top half of Bagel Thin and place on Hamburger.

Serve with your favorite side.

GRANNY'S GRILLED CHEESE

The Granny Smith originated in Eastwood, New South Wales, Australia in 1868. Its discoverer, Maria Ann Smith had migrated to the district from Beckley, East Sussex in 1838 with her husband Thomas. They purchased a small orchard in the area in 1855-1856 and began cultivating fruit, for which the area was a popular center in colonial Australia. Smith bore numerous children and was a prominent figure in the district, earning the nickname 'Granny' Smith in her advanced years.

INGREDIENTS

2 slices Whole Wheat or Whole Grain Bread
2 ½ ounces Reduced Fat Shredded Swiss cheese
½ Granny Smith apple, peeled, cored and thinly sliced
Olive Oil

DIRECTIONS

Heat a skillet on medium.

Brush one side of each slice of bread with Olive Oil.

Place 1 slice, Olive Oil side down into skillet and arrange Apple slices on top of it.

Sprinkle cheese over the Apple slices.

Top with remaining slice of bread, Olive Oil side up.

Cook until bread is golden brown, then flip and cook until other side is golden brown.

Slice in half and serve with your side of choice.

STOP THE SALT

GOING BACK TO CALI MELT

Swiss cheese is a generic name for several related varieties of North American cheese which resemble Emmental cheese, a yellow, medium-hard cheese that originated in the area around Emmental, in Switzerland. Some types of Swiss cheese have a distinctive appearance, as the blocks of the cheese are riddled with holes known as "eyes". Swiss cheese without eyes is known as "blind". Swiss cheese was also mentioned by the first century Roman historian Pliny the Elder, who called it Caseus Helveticus–the "cheese of the Helvetians", one of the tribes living in Switzerland at the time.

INGREDIENTS

2 slices Whole Grain Bread, lightly toasted
½ cup Mushrooms, sliced
½ Avocado, sliced
2 thick Tomato slices
2 slices Low Fat Swiss Cheese
2 ½ tablespoons toasted Almonds, sliced

DIRECTIONS

Preheat broiler.

Lay bread on a Baking Sheet.

Top each slice evenly with Tomato, Mushrooms, Avocado and Almonds.

Add a slice of Swiss to each piece of bread.

Broil until cheese melts and begins to bubble.

Serve with your side of choice.

SARDINEY THE GREEK

The Greek salad has been called the Rustic Salad and Summer Salad in Greek cuisine. The term Greek Salad is also used in North America, Australia, South Africa, and the United Kingdom to refer to a lettuce salad with Greek-inspired ingredients, dressed with oil and vinegar. Various other salads have also been called "Greek" in the English language in the last century, including some with no apparent connection to Greek cuisine. A 1925 Australian newspaper described a Greek Salad of boiled squash dressed with sour milk; a 1934 American newspaper described a mayonnaise-dressed lettuce salad with shredded cabbage and carrots.

INGREDIENTS

Can of low sodium Sardines, drained
¼ Cucumber, cut into chunks
Small Tomato, cut into chunks
⅛ Red Onion, thinly sliced
1 ounce Feta cheese
4 ounces low sodium Chickpeas, drained
1½ tablespoons Lemon Juice
1 tablespoon Olive Oil
½ Garlic clove, minced
1 teaspoon Oregano
Black Pepper

DIRECTIONS

Mix Lemon Juice, Oil, Garlic, Oregano and Pepper in a bowl.

Add remaining ingredients except Sardines and toss.

Plate and top with Sardines.

TACODS

The taco predates the arrival of Europeans in Mexico. There is anthropological evidence that the indigenous people living in the lake region of the Valley of Mexico traditionally ate tacos filled with small fish. Writing at the time of the Spanish conquistadors, Bernal Díaz del Castillo documented the first taco feast enjoyed by Europeans, a meal which Hernán Cortés arranged for his captains in Coyoacán. It is not clear why the Spanish used their word, "taco", to describe this indigenous food.

INGREDIENTS

Cod Fillet, cut into small pieces
3 Corn Tortillas
2 tablespoons Mayo
Dash of Cayenne Pepper
2 tablespoons Cilantro
1 tablespoon Olive Oil
1 tablespoon Lemon Juice
Shredded Cabbage
Roma Tomato, chopped
Tabasco Sauce, to taste

DIRECTIONS

Combine Cod, Lemon Juice, Oil and Cilantro in bowl and mix.

Stir Mayo and Cilantro in a small bowl.

Add Cod mixture to a skillet and cook over medium-high heat for 6 to 7 minutes.

Evenly spread Mayo mixture on each Tortilla.

Fill Tortillas with Cod Mixture and add Cabbage, Tomatoes and Tabasco.

Serve with your favorite side.

PATRICIA MELT: HIGH SOCIETY BURGER

Rumor has it that the Patty Melt was created by William "Tiny" Naylor sometime in the 40's or 50's at his chain of Southern California coffee shops called Tiny Naylor's. In other places, especially in the U.S., a patty melt can consist of only the patty of a hamburger, with cheese, on a single piece of toast/bun. The sandwich is then fried with butter on a frying pan so that the cheese melts thoroughly. A patty melt, being a toasted and pressed sandwich, may also be considered a type of panini. In Belarus the addition of fish roe and chicken egg is common.

INGREDIENTS

4 ounce premade Hamburger Patty
2 slices Whole Wheat or 8 Grain Bread
½ Yellow Onion, cut into strips
2 slices Low Fat Swiss Cheese
Unsalted Butter
Olive Oil

DIRECTIONS

Add Oil to a skillet and heat on medium. Cook onions for 8 minutes until browned and tender.

Remove Onions and reserve and add a little more Oil to skillet.

Add Hamburger to the pan and cook for 3 to 4 minutes until browned. Flip and repeat then remove.

Butter the top and bottom outsides of the bread.

Top bottom bread with Cheese, Burger, Onions and other piece of Cheese. Top with other slice of bread.

Grill until golden and the cheese melts, about 3 to 4 minutes on each side.

Cut in half, plate and serve with side of choice.

TECHNICALLY IT'S FILLET-O-FISH

The Filet-O-Fish sandwich was created by a McDonald's franchise owner in Cincinnati, Ohio, named Lou Groen in 1962. Groen owned a McDonald's in a predominantly Roman Catholic neighborhood where his Catholic customers engaged in the practice of not eating meat on Fridays. The sandwich was the first non-hamburger menu item brought in by new McDonald's company owner Ray Kroc. Kroc made a deal with Groen: they would sell two non-meat sandwiches on a Friday, Kroc's own Hula Burger (grilled pineapple with cheese on a cold bun) and the Filet-O-Fish, and whichever sold the most would be added to the permanent menu. The Filet-O-Fish "won hands down" and was added to menus throughout 1963 until reaching nationwide status in 1965.

INGREDIENTS

4 ounce Tilapia Fillet
2 slices Whole Wheat or 8 Grain Bread
1 slice Swiss cheese
2 tablespoons Low Fat Mayo
2 tablespoons Red Onion, finely chopped
¼ Tomato, finely chopped
Dash of crushed Red Pepper
Black Pepper
Olive Oil

DIRECTIONS

Stir together Mayo, Onion, Tomato, Red Pepper and Black Pepper.

Heat Olive Oil in a skillet over medium heat.

Cook Tilapia for 4 to 5 minutes on each side until fish starts to flake.

Place slice of Cheese on top of the fillet, cover and cook until cheese is melted.

Place Fish on slice of bread, spread with sauce and top with other slice of bread.

Serve with side of choice.

SAMMIES & SUCH

JIVE TURKEY BURGER

Turkey burgers might seem like recent inventions but in fact they were found in California restaurants as early as 1938. Storing, roasting, and slicing turkey, as well as dealing with the carcass was a nuisance to restaurants, so turkey sandwiches were something of a rarity before WWII. In the 1950s boneless turkey rolls became available. They made it convenient for any restaurant to offer triple deckers with turkey (instead of chicken as previously) or turkey dinner specials with sliced white meat and gravy that undoubtedly came from a can.

INGREDIENTS

4 ounce premade Turkey Burger
1 slice Swiss cheese
10 slices of Mushroom
¼ small Yellow Onion, sliced thinly
Whole Wheat Sandwich Slim
1 tablespoon Low Fat Mayo

DIRECTIONS

Heat Olive Oil in a skillet over medium heat.

Add Turkey Burger and cook for 5-7 minutes on each side.

Heat Olive Oil in another skillet over medium heat.

Add Mushrooms and Onions. Saute until tender.

Place cooked Onions and Mushrooms on Burger and top with Swiss. Cook until melted.

Place Burger on Sandwich Slim. Add Mayo to top piece.

Serve with side of choice.

ELVIS HAS LEFT HIS SANDWICH

The peanut butter and banana sandwich has been referred to as a favorite of Elvis Presley who was renowned for his food cravings such as the Fool's Gold Loaf, a loaf of Italian bread filled with a pound of bacon, peanut butter, and grape jelly. Books on Elvis Presley's favorite foods and culinary tastes, as well as other published reports on his taste for peanut butter and banana sandwiches with or without bacon, have made the sandwich widely associated with Presley. It is often referred to using his name.

INGREDIENTS

2 tablespoons Unsalted Peanut Butter
1 Banana, sliced
2 slices Whole Wheat or 8 Grain Bread
Cooking Spray

DIRECTIONS

Heat a skillet over medium heat and coat with Cooking Spray.

Spread 1 Tablespoon of Peanut Butter onto each slice of bread.

Place Banana slices onto Peanut Butter side of one slice and top with other slice.

Press together firmly and fry Sandwich until golden brown, about 3 minutes per side.

Cut in half and serve with Grapes or sliced Apples.

ISLE OF CAPRESE SANDWICH

Mozzarella is a fresh cheese, originally from southern Italy, traditionally made from Italian buffalo and later cow's milk by the pasta filata method. The term is used for several kinds of Italian cheeses that are made using spinning and then cutting. (Hence the name, as the Italian verb mouncezare means "to cut".) Another type is Bocconcino. They are small mouncezarella cheeses the size of an egg. Like other mouncezarellas, they are semi-soft, white and rindless mild cheeses which originated in Naples.

INGREDIENTS

2 ounces Low Fat Mozzarella Cheese, sliced
3 slices of Tomato
⅛ cup Basil leaves, chopped
1 Sandwich Slim
Olive Oil
Black Pepper

DIRECTIONS

Layer sliced Tomatoes and Mozzarella on bottom of the Slim.

Sprinkle Basil on sandwich.

Drizzle with Olive Oil and season with Pepper.

Serve with side of choice.

STOP THE SALT

TERI YAKI PROM QUEEN

Teriyaki is a cooking technique used in Japanese cuisine in which foods are broiled or grilled while being basted in a marinade based on soy sauce, mirin, and sugar. The word teriyaki derives from the noun teri which refers to a shine or luster given by the sugar content in the teri, and yaki, which refers to the cooking method of grilling or broiling. Traditionally the meat is dipped in or brushed with sauce several times during cooking.

INGREDIENTS

Boneless, skinless Chicken Breast
2 slices Pineapple
4 Red Onion slices
Lettuce
1 slice Swiss cheese
2 slices Whole Wheat bread, lightly toasted
2 tablespoons no sodium added Teriyaki Marinade

DIRECTIONS

Brush Chicken with Marinade and let sit for 15 minutes.

Heat Olive Oil in a skillet over medium heat.

Place Chicken in skillet and cook, covered, 6 to 7 minutes on each side.

Add Cheese and cook until it's melted.

Place Chicken on bottom slice of bread. Top with Pineapple, then Lettuce and then Onion.

Place top slice of bread on sandwich and cut in half.

Serve with your side of choice.

WANGO MANGO QUESODILLIO

Quesadillas are basically toasted tortillas with cheese (queso is cheese in Spanish) inside. The name in Spanish literally means "little cheesy thing." What constitutes a quesadilla varies greatly between the U.S and Mexico and there is no universal agreement among chefs about them. They agree that the quesadilla and taco or burrito are different; the former being cooked after being filled or stuffed while the latter two are filled with pre-cooked ingredients. Also they may be made with flour, corn or wheat tortillas as well as Mexican Masa (tamale version.) The specific origin for the quesadilla was in colonial Mexico. The quesadilla as a food changed and evolved over many years as people experimented with different variations of it

INGREDIENTS

4 6 inch Corn Tortillas
3 ounces Low Fat Cream Cheese, softened
¼ Mango, peeled and diced
¼ Poblano Pepper, seeded and minced
1 tablespoon Unsalted Butter, melted

DIRECTIONS

Place frying pan over medium heat.

Spread 2 of the Tortillas with 1½ Tablespoon of Cream Cheese each.

Sprinkle Mango and Poblanos over Cheese.

Press the other Tortillas on top.

Brush butter on outside of Tortillas, top and bottom.

Cook for 5 minutes on each side or until golden brown.

Serve with your favorite side.

STOP THE SALT

EGGCADO NOT SHARKNADO

Here are some fun Avocado facts. In Brazil avocados mixed in with ice cream is a very popular dessert. The avocado is also called an Alligator Pear because of its pear-like shape and its bumpy green skin. The oldest living avocado tree is found on the University of California, Berkeley campus and was planted in 1879. Over 5% of all avocados are sold in the 2 weeks leading into the Super Bowl. That's a lot of avocados! Wow, pretty cool!

INGREDIENTS

1 Avocado, halved and pitted
2 Eggs
Black Pepper to taste
Pinch of Cayenne Pepper
1 tablespoon chopped fresh chives

DIRECTIONS

Preheat oven to 425

Place Avocado in baking dish and scoop some flesh out.

Crack 1 egg in each Avocado half.

Sprinkle with black pepper and cayenne pepper.

Cook for about 15 minutes or until your liking.

Top with chives and serve with fresh fruit.

HEY, HEY, HEY…CEVICHE!

The origin of ceviche is disputed. Possible origin sites for the dish include the western coast of north-central South America, or in Central America. The invention of the dish is also attributed to other coastal societies, such as the Polynesian islands of the south Pacific. The Spanish, who brought from Europe citrus fruits, such as lime, could have also originated the dish with roots in Moorish cuisine. However, the most likely origin lies in the area of present-day Peru. But who cares as long as we can enjoy it!

INGREDIENTS

⅓ pound of Sea Scallops, quartered
2 small Radishes, thinly sliced
⅓ Jalapeno, minced
¼ pint of Grape Tomatoes, quartered
¼ cup of Orange Juice
¼ cup of Lime Juice
2-3 small Corn Tortillas
½ Avocado, sliced

DIRECTIONS

Toss Scallops, Radishes, Jalapeno, Tomatoes, Orange Juice and Lime Juice in a glass bowl. Cover tightly with plastic wrap and refrigerate, stirring once, four to six hours.

Divide Ceviche on Tortillas and top with sliced Avocado.

Serve with sliced Red Pepper.

STOP THE SALT

PASTARAMA AND OTHER HITS

PONCE DE LEON PASTA

Ponce De Leon was a Spanish conquistador and explorer who was the first to discover and explore Florida and this recipe uses a Spanish onion…Coincidence? A Spanish onion is an onion that is typically about the size of a softball, has a fine grain, and a yellow or white skin. It's known for its very mild flavor, with some people finding it sweet enough to eat raw. Though Spanish onions don't keep that great, they work well in many different types of dishes. They are also popular with home gardeners, since they produce a lot of fruit but are pretty low maintenance.

INGREDIENTS

Shrimp, shelled and deveined
2 Roma Tomatoes
¼ Red Onion
¼ cup Spanish Onion
½ Clove of Garlic
½ tablespoon Unsalted Butter
½ tablespoon Crushed Red Pepper
½ tablespoon No Sodium Original Flavor Seasoning
Olive Oil
1 cup Linguine

DIRECTIONS

Add butter to Frying Pan and heat to bubbling.

Mince Garlic and add that and Shrimp. Sprinkle with Original Flavor Seasoning and cook for 4 minute or until Shrimp are opaque.

Remove Shrimp and set aside.

Add Olive Oil to pan and then sauté the Onions until tender. Chop Tomatoes and then add them and Crushed Red Pepper.

Cook over medium heat for 3-5 minutes, stirring occasionally.

Add Shrimp and heat for 1 minute.

Serve over Linguine, prepared per instructions.

RASTA PASTA SALAD

The traditional colors of Rastafarians are Red, Gold and Green which will also make up the colors of this awesome Pasta Salad. (They occasionally use black too, but hard to find an ingredient of that color.) The Rastafarian colors are very commonly sported on Rastafarian flag, badges and posters. The green, gold and red are the colors of the Ethiopian flag and show the loyalty Rastafari feel towards the Ethiopian state in the reign of King Selassie. The red, black and green were the colors used to represent Africa by the Marcus Garvey movement. Red is said to signify the blood of martyrs, green the vegetation and beauty of Ethiopia, and gold the wealth of Africa.

INGREDIENTS

1 cup Rotini Pasta
¼ pound Broccoli Crowns, cut to bite size
½ Red Pepper, chopped into small pieces
¼ Yellow Squash, cut into small medallions then cut four ways
3 tablespoons Low Sodium Balsamic Vinaigrette
Black Pepper

DIRECTIONS

Cook Pasta per instructions. Drain and put back in pot.

Add the Raw Vegetables, Black Pepper and Salad Dressing. Toss.

Plate on Pasta Bowl or Dinner Plate and put in the refrigerator for 30 minutes.

OLD SCHOOL FETTUCINE ALFREDO

Most restaurants serve this dish with a creamier version of the sauce which is traditional. It was named by an Italian restaurateur, Alfredo Di Lelio, at his restaurant Alfredo on the Via della Scrofa in Rome in 1914. A long-time customer recounted that Di Lelio's restaurant became famous when Mary Pickford and Douglas Fairbanks stopped in and fell in love with the dish while on their honeymoon in 1920. To express their gratitude, they gave him a golden fork and spoon along with a photo of them eating in his restaurant. He proudly displayed the photo on the wall. Pickford and Fairbanks served his dish to their friends and associates when they returned to Hollywood and word about the new dish quickly spread

INGREDIENTS

1¼ cups of Fettuccine Pasta
¼ cup Unsalted Butter, softened
¼ cup grated Parmesan Cheese
Black Pepper

DIRECTIONS

Prepare Pasta per instructions.

Drain and return to pot.

Top with pieces of butter and the cheese. Toss pasta until coated.

Season with Black Pepper and serve.

MISHITY MASH HAMMITY HASH

In Northern England, Corned Beef Hash is a traditional cheap and quick dish dating back many years. Corned Beef is nearly always from a can and almost always imported from South America. Canned corned beef was available more plentifully during war years when fresh meat was heavily rationed and became a staple food in the armed forces. The meal is made with that, stirred with browned onions, before having liquid added (either gravy or stock, or tinned tomatoes) then having lightly boiled sliced potatoes layered over the top before being browned under a hot grill. Some recipes would add peas or carrots. (Boring! Here is a cooler recipe.)

INGREDIENTS

¼ Green Bell Pepper, diced
¼ Red Bell Pepper, diced
¼ Medium Onion, diced
1 ounce Low Sodium Ham, diced
¾ cups Frozen Diced Hash Brown Potatoes, thawed
Sodium Free Cajun Seasoning
Black Pepper
Olive Oil

DIRECTIONS

Put Olive Oil in Frying Pan and cook at medium heat.

Add Peppers and Onion and cook around 5 minutes until tender, stirring occasionally.

Stir in Ham and cook an additional 2 minutes, until heated through.

Mix in Hash Browns and Cajun Seasoning. Cook without stirring for 4 minutes or until bottom is brown.

Stir again then cook without stirring for 4 minutes or until bottom is brown.

Stir in Black Pepper and plate.

STOP THE SALT

ARUGULA, GOAT AND A KID NAMED PASTA

When Steve Martin's character (in witness relocation) in the movie "My Blue Heaven" was asked what Arugula was, he responded, "It's a veg-a-tab-le!" Arugula, also known as rocket salad is a nutritious green-leafy vegetable of Mediterranean origin. Arugula is a quick growing and cool season crop whose leaves are ready to harvest within 40 days of sowing the seed and is an excellent source of all kinds of nutrition.

INGREDIENTS

6 ounces Rotini pasta
½ (7.5 ounces) can Cannellini Beans, drained
1½ ounces crumbled Goat Cheese
4 ounces Arugula, torn
¼ Red Onion, thinly sliced
3 tablespoons Low Sodium Balsamic Pepper
Black Pepper

DIRECTIONS

Cook pasta as directed. Drain and toss with Cannellini Beans and Goat Cheese.

Add Arugula and Red Onion to mixture. Pour in dressing and toss all ingredients.

Plate and top with Black Pepper.

IT'S PRONOUNCED KEEN-WA AND CHEESE

I know it is spelled Quinoa but sounds nothing like that. (Just like the singer Sade.) It's a species of goosefoot *(Chenopodium)* and is a grain-like crop grown primarily for its edible seeds. It is a pseudocereal rather than a true cereal, or grain, as it is not a member of the true grass family. As a chenopod, quinoa is closely related to species such as beets, spinach and tumbleweeds.

INGREDIENTS

¾ cup Quinoa
1½ ounces Fat-Free Plain Yogurt
½ teaspoon Dijon or Spicy Mustard
¼ cup Low-Fat Shredded Cheddar Cheese
1 Roma Tomato
½ Green Pepper

DIRECTIONS

Prepare Quinoa as directed. When it's cooking, clean Green Pepper and then chop it and the Roma Tomato.

When done cooking add Yogurt and Mustard to the Quinoa. Stir in completely and then mix in Cheese.

Add raw, chopped Veggie and mix again.

SQUASH THE ROTINI

Rotini is a type of helix or corkscrew shaped pasta. The name is supposed to derive from the Italian for twists, but the word "rotini" does not exist in Italian. It is related to fusilli, but has a tighter helix with a smaller pitch. It should not be confused with rotelle ("wagon wheel" pasta). Rotini originated from Northern Italy and the tight twists help them retain a wide variety of sauces better. In the US they may also be called "Scroodle," "Scroodle Noodles", "Scrotini", "Skroodle", "Scroodle Macaroni", or "corkscrews".

INGREDIENTS

Rotini
1 small Yellow Squash
5 ounces Frozen Peas
2 tablespoons unsalted Butter, cut into small pieces
¼ cup grated Parmesan Cheese
2 teaspoons Lemon Juice
2 tablespoons Basil
Black Pepper

DIRECTIONS

Cook the Rotini for 2 minutes.

Add Squash and Peas and cook for 2 more minutes.

Reserve ¼ cup of Pasta Water.

Drain Pasta mixture and return to pot.

Add Butter, Lemon Juice, ⅛ cup Parmesan and Pasta Water to pot.

Add Pepper and toss to combine.

Stir in Basil and sprinkle with remaining Parmesan Cheese.

POLLO PENNE WITH OTHER GOOD STUFF

Penne is a type of pasta with cylinder-shaped pieces. Penne is the plural form of the Italian penna, deriving from Latin penna (meaning "feather" or "quill") and is a cognate of the English word pen. In Italy, penne are produced in two main variants: "penne lisce" (smooth) and "penne rigate" (furrowed), the latter having ridges on each penna. There is also pennoni ("big quills"), which is a wider version of penne.

INGREDIENTS

7 ounce Whole Wheat Penne
Boneless, Skinless Chicken Breast, cut into cubes
¼ cup Low Sodium Chicken Broth
6 Asparagus Spears, cut in half
½ cup Mushrooms, sliced
Small Roma Tomato, chopped
Olive Oil
Black Pepper

DIRECTIONS

Pour Olive Oil in frying pan over medium heat.

Add Chicken and cook until partially done.

Add Asparagus and Mushrooms and continue cooking until Chicken is done.

Add Chicken Broth, cover and cook until Asparagus is crisp and tender.

Add cooked Penne, dash of Black Pepper and remove from heat.

Top off with Roma Tomato.

CCV FOR YOU AND ME (COUS COUS, CHICKEN AND VEGGIES)

One of the earliest references to couscous in France is in Brittany, in a letter dated January 12, 1699. But it made an earlier appearance in Provence, where the traveler Jean-Jacques Bouchard wrote of eating it in Toulon in 1630. Couscous was originally made from millet.[5] Historians have different opinions as to when wheat began to replace the use of millet. The conversion seems to have occurred sometime in the 20th century, although many regions continue to use the traditional millet. Couscous seems to have a North African origin. Archaeological evidence dating back to the 10th century, consisting of kitchen utensils needed to prepare this dish, has been found in this part of the world.

INGREDIENTS

½ Cup Cous Cous
1 Boneless, Skinless Chicken Breast, cooked and cubed
¼ Red Onion, sliced
¼ Green Bell Pepper, seeded and sliced
¼ Carrot, sliced in the coin shaped slices
Olive Oil

DIRECTIONS

Heat Olive Oil in Frying Pan on medium.

Add Onion, Bell Pepper and Carrots and saute until softened.

Add Chicken and Cous Cous to heat through.

Serve when warmed.

IS IT TEX? IS IT MEX? OR IS IT TEX-MEX? ONLY THE QUINOA KNOWS

The word "Tex-Mex" first entered the English language as a nickname for the Texas Mexican Railway, chartered in southern Texas in 1875. In train schedules published in the newspapers of the 1800s the names of railroads were abbreviated. The Missouri Pacific was called the Mo. Pac. and the Texas-Mexican was abbreviated Tex. Mex. In the 1920s, the hyphenated form was used in American newspapers in reference to the railroad and to describe people of Mexican ancestry who were born in Texas.

INGREDIENTS

¾ Cup Quinoa
¼ cup Frozen Corn, cooked
¼ can of low sodium Black Beans, drained
1 Roma Tomato, chopped
¼ White Onion, chopped
½ Avocado, peeled and chopped into cubes
1 tablespoon Lemon Juice
2 tablespoons Olive Oil
Dash of Coriander
Dash of Cayenne Pepper
Black Pepper

DIRECTIONS

Mix 1 Tablespoon Olive Oil and Black Pepper with Quinoa.

In a separate bowl mix 1 Tablespoon Olive Oil and remaining ingredients.

Plate the Quinoa and top with the mixture.

CHICKEN OR ZO…YOU MAKE THE CALL

Orzo pasta is a type of pasta which is made in the shape of a grain of rice. The word orzo is Italian for "barley," and a reference to the size and shape of the pasta. You can also see orzo called kritharaki, manestra, rosa marina, reiskornpasta, or pasta gallo pion. This pasta is very popular in Greece especially, although it is used in other Mediterranean and Middle Eastern nations and in some parts of Germany as well.

INGREDIENTS

Boneless, Skinless Chicken Breast, cut into bite-sized pieces
7 ounces Orzo Pasta
1 cup Spinach Leaves
Olive Oil
⅛ teaspoon Crushed Red Pepper
1½ teaspoon of Parsley
1 clove Garlic, crushed

DIRECTIONS

Heat Olive Oil over medium-high heat.

Cook the Garlic and Red Pepper for 1 minute.

Stir in Chicken and cook for 5 minutes.

Reduce heat to medium and mix in cooked Orzo and Parsley.

Add Spinach and cook for 5 minutes stirring occasionally.

Serve with Crushed Black Pepper if desired.

SPEARING CHICKEN AND PENNE

Asparagus has been used as a vegetable and medicine, owing to its delicate flavor, diuretic properties, and more. It is pictured as an offering on an Egyptian frieze dating to 3000 BC. Still in ancient times, it was known in Syria and in Spain. Greeks and Romans ate it fresh when in season and dried the vegetable for use in winter; Romans would even freeze it high in the Alps, for the Feast of Epicurus. Emperor Augustus reserved the "Asparagus Fleet" for hauling the vegetable, and coined the expression "faster than cooking asparagus" for quick action.

INGREDIENTS

Boneless, Skinless Chicken Breast, cut into cubes
7 ounces Penne Pasta
¼ Cup Low Sodium Chicken Broth
4 ounces Asparagus spears, trimmed and cut into 1 inch pieces
Olive Oil
½ Clove Garlic, thinly sliced
Garlic Powder to taste
Black Pepper to taste

DIRECTIONS

Heat Olive Oil over medium-high heat.

Add Chicken, Black Pepper and Garlic Powder. Cook for around 5 minutes until Chicken is browned.

Remove Chicken and place on a Paper Towel.

Pour Chicken Broth in pan.

Stir in Asparagus, Garlic and a pinch more Garlic Powder.

Cover and steam for between 5 to 10 minutes until Asparagus is tender.

Return Chicken to skillet to warm through.

Stir mixture into Penne and mix well and let sit for 5 minutes.

Stir again and serve.

STOP THE SALT

NOT SCALLOPED POTATOES…SCALLOP TOMATOES

The scallop shell is the traditional emblem of James, son of Zebedee, and is popular with pilgrims on the Way of St James to the apostle's shrine at Santiago de Compostela in Galicia (Spain). Medieval Christians making the pilgrimage to his shrine often wore a scallop shell symbol on their hat or clothes. The pilgrim also carried a scallop shell with him, and would present himself at churches, castles, abbeys etc., where he could expect to be given as much sustenance as he could pick up with one scoop. Probably he would be given oats, barley, and perhaps beer or wine. Thus even the poorest household could give charity without being overburdened.

INGREDIENTS

7 ounces Fettuccine
4 ounces Bay Scallops
1 Roma Tomatoes, chopped
½ Zucchini, diced
1 Garlic clove, crushed
Olive Oil
¼ teaspoon Crushed Red Pepper flakes
2 ounce Basil

DIRECTIONS

Heat skillet on medium and add Olive Oil and Garlic. Cook until it's tender.

Add Zucchini, Pepper Flakes, Basil and sauté for 10 minutes.

Now toss in Tomatoes and Scallops and cook for 5 minutes until Scallops are opaque.

Pour mixture over Fettuccine and serve.

MARI NARA QUITE CONTRARA…SHE'S SPICY!

At least two folk theories are given as to the origin of Marinara sauce: One says cooks aboard Neapolitan ships invented marinara sauce in the mid-16th century after Spaniards introduced the tomato to Europe. The original recipe did not contain seafood, so it was resistant to spoilage due to the high acid content of tomatoes. This made it ideal for lengthy sea voyages hundreds of years before refrigeration methods were invented. Another theory states this was a sauce prepared by the wives of Neapolitan sailors upon their return from sea.

INGREDIENTS

6 large Shrimp, peeled and deveined
7 ounces Angel Hair Pasta
2 Garlic Clove, thinly sliced
¾ teaspoon crushed Red Pepper flakes
4–6 ounces No Salt Added or Low Sodium Pasta Sauce
Olive Oil

DIRECTIONS

Heat Olive Oil over medium-high heat.

Cook Shrimp for 4 to 5 minutes until golden brown and remove.

Add some more Olive Oil and Red Pepper and Garlic. Cook for around 1 minute.

Pour in Pasta Sauce and bring to a simmer.

Return Shrimp to pan and simmer for another minute.

Serve over the cooked Angel Hair Pasta.

NOT FUSILLI JERRY

Fusilli are long, thick, corkscrew shaped pasta. The word fusilli presumably comes from fuso, as traditionally it is "spun" by pressing and rolling a small rod over the thin strips of pasta to wind them around it in a corkscrew shape, much like a modern Turkish spindle. The pasta goes back a ways into ancient history, to 1550 in Granducato di Toscana, before Italy was a united country. It gained more recognition when Kramer made a small Fusilli Jerry statue on an episode of "Seinfeld".

INGREDIENTS

1 slice Turkey or Lower Sodium Bacon, cut into ½ inch pieces
7 ounces Fusilli
1 medium Yellow Squash, slice and quartered
1 clove Garlic, thinly sliced
1 ounce Grated Parmesan Cheese
¼ cup Heavy Cream
Black Pepper

DIRECTIONS

Heat skillet over medium and add Bacon.

Cook until crisp and brown around 5 to 7 minutes then place on a paper towel.

Turn skillet to medium-high and add Squash and Garlic to the left over Bacon fat.

Season with Pepper, cover and cook for 5 to 7 minutes, stirring occasionally.

Uncover and cook for 3 more minutes or until Squash is tender.

Add Cream and cooked Fusilli to skillet and toss well and cook until Cream starts to thicken.

Remove from heat. Stir in Parmesan Cheese and a teaspoon of water and stir.

Serve and top with the Bacon.

HEY, CACCIATORE (TO THE THEME OF HEY, MACARENA)

Cacciatore means "hunter's style". This dish developed in central Italy. It is considered a country-style dish in which chicken pieces are simmered together with tomatoes and mushrooms. The dish originated in the Renaissance period (1450-1600) when the only people who could afford to enjoy poultry and the sport of hunting were the well-to-do. There are many different variations of this dish based upon ingredients available in specific regions. For example, in southern Italy, cacciatore often includes red wine, while northern Italian chefs might use white wine.

INGREDIENTS

Boneless, Skinless Chicken Breast
7 ounces Spaghetti, cooked
¼ Green Pepper, seeded and cut into strips
¼ Red Onion, sliced into rings
2 ounces Mushrooms, sliced
4 ounces No Salt Added or Low Sodium Pasta Sauce
Dash of Basil
Dash or Oregano
Dash or Garlic Powder
Olive Oil

DIRECTIONS

Heat Olive Oil in a skillet over medium heat.

Add Green Pepper, Mushrooms and Onions and cook for 5 minutes until crisp and tender.

Place Chicken Breast on veggies.

In a small bowl combine Pasta Sauce and seasonings.

Pour over the Chicken and simmer for 20 minutes.

Serve on top of Spaghetti.

NOT TUNA SALAD, TUNA PASTA SALAD

According to legend, macaroni was brought to Italy by Marco Polo, returning to Venice from China in 1292. This hypothesis has long been disproved, since it seems that macaroni was already used in Italy at least a century before, like pasta in general; Moroccan geographer Muhammad al-Idrisi, who lived in Sicily, documented macaroni in Sicily and in particular in Trabia. In areas with large Chinese populations open to Western cultural influence, such as Hong Kong, Macao, Malaysia and Singapore, the local Chinese have adopted macaroni as an ingredient for Chinese-style Western cuisine.

INGREDIENTS

Can No Salt Added Tuna, drained
7 ounces Elbow Macaroni
¼ Zucchini, chopped
6-8 Cherry Tomatoes, halved
3 ounces Bagged Spinach
Olive Oil
Black Pepper

DIRECTIONS

Heat Olive Oil in frying pan over medium.

Cook Zucchini for about 5 minutes until crisp and tender.

Rinse Zucchini under cold water.

Rinse Macaroni under cold water.

Mix all ingredients together and top with Black Pepper.

Serve.

HAWAII QUIN-O

John Kidwell is credited with the introduction of the pineapple industry in Hawaii. Large-scale pineapple cultivation by U.S. companies began in the early 1900s on Hawaii. Among the most famous and influential pineapple industrialists was James Dole who moved to Hawaii in 1899 and started a pineapple plantation in 1900. Interesting facts, one pineapple plant produces only one pineapple every 2 years and can fruit for up to 50 years in the wild.

INGREDIENTS

4 Large Shrimp, each shelled and cut into three pieces
½ cup Quinoa, prepared
¼ cup canned crushed Pineapple
Olive Oil

DIRECTIONS

Place frying pan over medium heat and add Olive Oil.

Add Shrimp and Pineapple.

Stir both until they turn white and are cooked through.

Add Quinoa and heat until slightly browned.

QUINOA, QUESO & EL BROCOLI

Sure this title sounds like an ethnic dish, but it is whiter than a Dairy Farmer in Wisconsin. The word broccoli comes from the Latin word brachium and the Italian word braccio, which means "arm" and is part of the cabbage family. Also eating broccoli reduces the risk of coronary heart disease and death in postmenopausal women. But it's good for all of us!

INGREDIENTS

¾ cup of Quinoa
Broccoli
¼ cup Low Fat Shredded Swiss Cheese

DIRECTIONS

Prepare Quinoa as directed.

Chop up cooked Broccoli into small bite sized pieces.

Mix the two ingredients together in Quinoa pot and then mix in Swiss Cheese.

Serve on a Dinner Plate.

(You can also serve with Scrambled Egg Substitute for a great Breakfast.)

SOME SALADS & SOME SIDES

POPEYE SALAD

"I'm strong to the finish, cause' I eats my Spinach, I'm Popeye the sailor man! (toot, toot)"

Spinach originated in Persia, (modern day Iran). The earliest records of its cultivation go back 2,000 years. It was introduced to China in the 600's and to Spain around 1100. By the 16th century it was well established in Europe. The Spaniards brought it to America. Spinach was the first vegetable frozen and sold commercially. That honor goes to Clarence Birdseye in Springfield Massachusetts in 1930. Fresh spinach is available year round. California and Texas are the major growers.

INGREDIENTS

4 ounces Bagged Spinach
Hard Boiled Egg, sliced into small pieces
7-10 Grape Tomatoes
¼ Red Onion, chopped
½ cup Mushrooms, sliced
¼ cup Feta Cheese
Olive Oil
Ground Pepper

DIRECTIONS

Put Spinach in a bowl.

Add egg, onion, mushrooms and tomatoes to salad. Sprinkle on Feta Cheese.

Add Olive Oil to your taste and toss Salad. Top with crushed Black Pepper.

KALE CHIPS: SEE IT'S NOT JUST A GARNISH

Remember when Kale was something that displayed food at Buffet's? Well, things have changed! Kale is very high in beta carotene, vitamin K, vitamin C, and rich in calcium. Until the end of the Middle Ages, kale was one of the most common green vegetables in all of Europe and during World War II, the cultivation of kale in the U.K. was encouraged by the Dig for Victory campaign. So it has always been around but it just took a little time off.

INGREDIENTS

¼ Bunch of Kale
Olive Oil
Red Pepper Flakes
Or
Original No Sodium Seasoning
Black Pepper

DIRECTIONS

Preheat oven.

Put foil on Cooking Pan.

In a small bowl mix your choice of Seasoning and Black Pepper with Olive Oil.

Remove Kale leaves from stem and tear into bite sized pieces.

Place on pan and bake 10 – 15 minutes until edges are brown.

STOP THE SALT

YOU SAY GARBANZO SALAD, I SAY CHICKPEA SALAD

This isn't the East Coast versus West Coast Rap wars. Is it a chickpea or a garbanzo bean? It depends on where your culinary loyalties lie. If you're with the French and Italians, you may think of them as chiche and ceci, respectively. If you're with the Spanish, then you may know them as garbanzos. The English term is chickpea. But no matter what you call them, they are a helpful source of zinc, folate and protein.

INGREDIENTS

¼ small Eggplant, cut into chunks
2 Roma Tomatoes, chopped and cored
¼ Zucchini, cut into chunks
½ Red Pepper, cored, seeded and sliced
¾ cup of Low Sodium canned Chickpeas
Olive Oil
No Sodium Original flavored seasoning.

DIRECTIONS

Preheat Oven.

Put foil on Cooking Pan.

Combine Eggplant, Tomatoes, Zucchini, Bell Peppers and Olive Oil and place on pan.

Roast 35 minutes or until Veggies are tender and starting to brown.

Stir in Chickpeas and roast until heated through. (5 – 10 minutes.)

Serve in Pasta Bowl.

Top with Seasoning.

DIRTY STINKIN' RICE!

Dirty rice is a traditional Cajun dish made from white rice cooked with small pieces of chicken liver or giblets, which give it a dark and dirty color and a mild but distinctive flavor. It's similar to a pilaf, and includes green bell pepper, celery and onion. It is most common in the Cajun regions of southern Louisiana and Mississippi and in some southern regions it is also called rice dressing. Well, I'm not in a southern region and that sounds too complicated for a side. So here's my recipe.

INGREDIENTS

1 cup Brown Rice, cooked
1 Roma Tomato, seeded and chopped
2 tablespoons Crushed Red Pepper
2 teaspoons Spicy Mustard
Olive Oil

DIRECTIONS

Heat Olive Oil in pan over medium heat.

Add Olive Oil, Tomatoes and Crushed Red Pepper. Cook for 2 minutes.

Add Rice and Mustard. Reduce to low heat and stir often until warm all the way through.

CUCU TOMMY SALAD

Refreshing side salads make a lunch enjoyable. Cucumbers are cool and moist due to their high water content and belong to the same family as pumpkins, zucchini, watermelon and other squashes. Cucumbers are also low in fat, sodium, and calories and are a good source of Vitamin C, Vitamin K and Potassium. In addition the green color of cucumber skin indicates it is a great source of chlorophyll, which is a valuable phytonutrient. Now that's good eating!

INGREDIENTS

¼ Cucumber
1 Roma Tomato
2 tablespoons Lower Sodium Balsamic Vinaigrette
Black Pepper
No Sodium Original Seasoning Blend

DIRECTIONS

Cut Cucumber and Tomato into small pieces and place in a bowl.

Add Vinaigrette and Pepper and Seasoning to taste. Stir together.

Refrigerate for an hour.

For this recipe you can double or triple the ingredients if you want to make for a few days.

SOME SALADS & SOME SIDES

UMA…OKRA… OKRA…UMA

Okra is a popular health food due to its high fiber, vitamin C, and folate content. Okra is also known for being high in antioxidants. Okra is also a good source of calcium and potassium. The geographical origin of okra is disputed, with supporters of South Asian, Ethiopian and West African origins. Supporters of a South Asian origin point to the presence of its proposed parents in that region. Supporters of a West African origin point to the greater diversity of okra in that region.

INGREDIENTS

15-20 pieces of Frozen Okra, tops snipped off
½ cup Low Sodium Bread Crumbs
2 tablespoons Zesty No Sodium Seasoning
Black Pepper
Olive Oil

DIRECTIONS

Preheat Oven.

Put foil on a Cooking Pan.

Mix Bread Crumbs, Seasoning and Pepper and put in a Ziploc bag.

Toss Okra in Olive Oil until covered.

Drop Okra in bag and shake until coated with Bread Crumb mixture.

Put on Pan and cook for around 30 minutes or until browned, turning half way through.

STOP THE SALT

YOU DOWN WITH C.C.S.? (CRUNCHY CUCUMBER SALAD)

This great side dish has Cilantro in it which is an herb with wide delicate lacy green leaves and a pungent flavor. The seed of the cilantro plant is known as coriander. Although cilantro and coriander come from the same plant, their flavors are very different and cannot be substituted for each other. All parts of the plant are edible, but the fresh leaves and the dried seeds are the most commonly used in cooking.

INGREDIENTS

1 Cucumber, diced
¼ Red Onion, diced fine
1 stalk Celery, diced
⅛ cup chopped Cilantro
½ Jalapeno, seeds removed and minced
1 lime
1 tablespoon Olive Oil
Black Pepper

DIRECTIONS

Mix Lime Juice, Pepper and Olive Oil in mixing bowl.

Add remaining ingredients and toss.

Serve chilled.

SOME SALADS & SOME SIDES

POPPIN' POTATO ROSTI

Rosti is a Swiss dish consisting mainly of potatoes. It was originally a common breakfast eaten by farmers in the canton of Bern, but today is eaten all over Switzerland and also in many restaurants in the western world. Many Swiss people consider rosti a national dish. Today, rather than considering it a complete breakfast, it is more commonly served to accompany other dishes. It is also a dish one can order in most restaurants to replace the standard side dish of any given meal.

INGREDIENTS

1 large Russet Potato, peeled and grated
2 teaspoons Parsley
2 teaspoons Tarragon
2 teaspoons Crushed Red Pepper
1 teaspoon Cayenne Pepper
2 tablespoons Olive Oil

DIRECTIONS

Squeeze as much liquid out of potato as possible.

Place in bowl and toss with Parsley, Tarragon and Peppers.

Heat 1 tablespoon of Olive Oil in pan over medium heat.

Press Potato mixture into pan and cook 10 minutes.

Remove from pan and add other tablespoon of Olive Oil.

Flip Rosti back into pan, browned side up and cook for 10 more minutes.

GRAB A CAB SALAD
(CELERY, AVOCADO AND BELL PEPPER)

Generally, any food that's good for your body is good for your breath, but celery seems custom made for fighting halitosis. Munching on a stalk of celery is helpful in two ways: its roughness helps scrub bacteria from the back of the tongue and its natural fibers assist in cleaning the teeth. It's like using an edible toothbrush. In fact, if you ever find yourself without a toothbrush, chomping on a celery stick after a meal or first thing in the morning will do the trick.

INGREDIENTS

1 stalk Celery, diced
¼ Red Bell Pepper, cleaned and diced
½ Avocado, skinned and diced
2 tablespoons low sodium Vinaigrette
Black Pepper

DIRECTIONS

Combine Celery, Bell Pepper and Avocado in a bowl.

Add Vinaigrette and Black Pepper.

Toss together.

GREENIE ZUCHINNI

Green beans, also known as French beans, Fine beans (British English), string beans in the northeastern and western United States, or ejotes in Mexico, are the unripe fruit of specific cultivated varieties of the common bean. Green bean varieties have been bred especially for the fleshiness, flavor, or sweetness of their pods. Haricots verts, French for "green beans", may refer to a longer, thinner type of green bean than the typical American green bean. The first "stringless" bean was bred in 1894 by Calvin Keeney, called the "father of the stringless bean", while working in Le Roy, New York.

INGREDIENTS

¼ pound Green Beans, cooked and stemmed
½ small Zucchini, julienned
2 tablespoons Low Sodium Vinaigrette
1 teaspoon Capers, rinsed and chopped
Black Pepper
Basil

DIRECTIONS

Rinse Green Beans under cold water and cut in half.

Add to a bowl with Zucchini.

Add dressing to the two.

Mix in Capers, Black Pepper and Basil.

CORNO COBBO MEXICALI STYLE

Actually that isn't the way you say Corn on the Cob in Spanish. It's actually called Elote. It's a popular street food in Mexico, although they are frequently served at home prepared in the same way (boiled in husk). In Mexico, Chicago, and the southern U.S., it is customary to consume elotes on a stick, or by grasping the husk of the cob that has been pulled down to form a "handle". Another way of presenting elotes is by serving the cut kernels in a bowl. In the southern and central areas of Mexico, people call this esquites instead of elote.

INGREDIENTS

1 Ear of Corn husked then cooked
½ ounce grated Parmesan
½ tablespoon Unsalted Butter
½ tablespoon Reduced Fat Mayo
⅛ teaspoon Chili Powder
Ground Black Pepper

DIRECTIONS

Remove Corn from microwave and brush with Butter followed by Mayo.

Roll in Parmesan to coat.

Sprinkle with Chili Powder and Black Pepper.

Serve.

SOME SALADS & SOME SIDES

CAKA SALAD

Kale is a vegetable with green or purple leaves, in which the central leaves do not form a head. It is considered to be closer to wild cabbage than most domesticated forms. Until the end of the Middle Ages, kale was one of the most common green vegetables in all of Europe. Curly leafed varieties of cabbage already existed along with flat leafed varieties in Greece in the fourth century BC. During World War II, the cultivation of kale in the U.K. was encouraged by the Dig for Victory campaign. The vegetable was easy to grow and provided important nutrients to supplement those missing from a normal diet because of rationing.

INGREDIENTS

¼ Bunch of Kale, sliced with bottom stem removed
¼ Avocado, peeled
½ of a Lemon
1 clove of Garlic, crushed
⅛ Sweet Onion, chopped
¼ any Red Apple, chopped
1 ounce Unsalted Cashews

DIRECTIONS

Put sliced Kale in a bowl.

Add Avocado and then add juice from the Lemon.

With your fingers massage Avocado into the Kale until it is no longer chunky and leaves are coated.

Add Garlic, Onion and Apple. Stir well.

Plate and top with Cashews.

CHICKA, CHICKA, CHICKABEE SALAD

Chickpeas have been around forever. By the Bronze Age, chickpeas were known in Italy and Greece. In classical Greece, they were called erébinthos and eaten as a staple, a dessert, or consumed raw when young. The Romans knew several varieties such as venus, ram and punic chickpeas. They were both cooked down into a broth and roasted as a snack. The Roman gourmet Apicius gives several recipes for chickpeas. Carbonized chickpeas have been found at the Roman legion fort at Neuss, Germany in layers from the first century CE, along with rice.

INGREDIENTS

3 ounces canned Low Sodium Chickpeas, drained
1 small Roma Tomato, chopped
¼ Celery stalk, chopped
¼ Cucumber chopped
¼ Red Bell Pepper, seeded and chopped
1 ounce crumbled Feta Cheese
1 tablespoon Lemon Juice
1 tablespoon Olive Oil
1 teaspoon Dried Oregano

DIRECTIONS

Mix up Chickpeas, Vegetables and Feta Cheese in a bowl.

Add Lemon Juice and Olive Oil.

Sprinkle with Oregano.

Refrigerate until chilled.

SOME SALADS & SOME SIDES

A SHRIMPY SALAD (BUT NOT IN SIZE)

Bet you didn't know these facts about Shrimp. A. Every shrimp is actually born a male and then become females as they mature. B. Some shrimp can live as long as six and a half years, while some only live about a year or so. C. One billion pounds of shrimp are eaten every year by Americans. D. A shrimp can average about 6 inches while the longest ever found was at 16 inches. E. May 9th is National Shrimp Day. OK, now you're ready for Jeopardy.

INGREDIENTS

6 large Shrimp
6 ounces bagged Spinach
½ Hard Boiled Egg, chopped
¼ Red Bell Pepper, seeded and sliced into strips
¼ Yellow Bell Pepper, seeded and sliced into strips
2 or 3 Baby Bella Mushrooms, sliced
2 tablespoons low sodium Balsamic Vinaigrette
Olive Oil

INGREDIENTS

Heat Olive Oil in a frying pan over medium heat.

Add Shrimp and cook for 2 minutes on each side or until they become white.

Mix up Spinach, Bell Peppers, Mushroom and Eggs in a bowl.

Add Vinaigrette and toss.

Plate and then place Shrimp on top.

Add ground Black Pepper if desired.

STOP THE SALT

WHAT'S EATING CHICKEN GRAPE?

Here are some facts about Grapes to increase your knowledge. A. America's oldest grapevine is 400 years old and is in North Carolina. B. While grapes are 80% water, when they become raisins the water content is just 15%. C. You can get about 15,000 glasses of wine from an acre of grapes. D. About a quarter of the grapes used in the US come from Chile. E. Grapes have been thought to have healing properties since ancient times.

INGREDIENTS

1 boneless, skinless Chicken Breast, cooked and chopped up
½ cup Green Seedless Grapes, sliced
1 ounce Chopped Walnuts
1 tablespoon Low Fat Mayo
4 ounces Baby Greens
1 tablespoon Balsamic Vinaigrette

DIRECTIONS

Mix Chicken, Grapes, Walnuts and Mayo.

Toss Baby Greens with Vinaigrette.

Place Baby Greens on a plate and top with Chicken mixture.

LEE J. OR TY COBB SALAD…THE CHOICE IS YOURS

Various stories of how the Cobb salad was invented exist. The most popular one says that it came about in the 1930s at the Hollywood Brown Derby restaurant, where it became a signature dish. It is named for the restaurant's owner, Robert Howard Cobb. Stories vary as to whether the salad was invented by Cobb or by his chef, Chuck Wilson. The legend is that Cobb had not eaten until near midnight, and so he mixed together leftovers he found in the kitchen, along with some bacon cooked by the line cook, and tossed it with their French dressing.

INGREDIENTS

Chicken Breast, Cooked and chopped up
7 ounces bagged Iceberg/Romaine mix
1 Egg, hard-boiled, peeled and chopped
1 Roma Tomato, diced
¼ Cucumber, sliced
¼ Avocado, diced
1 piece of Bacon, crumbled
1 ounce crumbled Blue Cheese
3 tablespoons low sodium Balsamic Vinaigrette
Black Pepper

DIRECTIONS

Place Lettuce in bowl.

Add ½ the dressing and toss to coat.

Plate the Lettuce.

Arrange remaining ingredients on top of the Lettuce.

Drizzle the rest of the dressing and add Black Pepper.

STOP THE SALT

SUM, SUM, SUMMERTIME, SUM, SUM, SUMMERTIME SALAD!

The Peach was brought to the Americas by Spanish explorers in the 16th century, and eventually made it to England and France in the 17th century, where it was a prized and expensive treat. The horticulturist George Minifie supposedly brought the first peaches from England to its North American colonies in the early 17th century, planting them at his Estate of Buckland in Virginia. Although Thomas Jefferson had peach trees at Monticello, United States farmers did not begin commercial production until the 19th century in Maryland, Delaware, Georgia and finally Virginia.

INGREDIENTS

7 ounces Baby Greens
1 small Peach, pit removed and sliced
1 ounce crumbled Goat Cheese
1 tablespoon Olive Oil
2 teaspoon Red Wine Vinegar
½ teaspoon Honey
Dash of Tarragon, Parsley or Basil
Black Pepper

DIRECTIONS

Combine Olive Oil, Vinegar and Honey.

Add the Baby Greens and toss well.

Place on plate and tops with Peaches, Goat Cheese and Herbs.

Use Black Pepper to season.

LEAN MEAN GREEN BEAN SALAD

Because of their rich green color, we don't always think about green beans as providing us with important amounts of colorful pigments like carotenoids. But they do! Recent studies have confirmed the presence of lutein, beta-carotene, violaxanthin, and neoxanthin in green beans. In some cases, the presence of these carotenoids in green beans is comparable to their presence in other carotenoid-rich vegetables like carrots and tomatoes. The only reason we don't see these carotenoids is because of the concentrated chlorophyll content of green beans and the amazing shades of green that it provides.

INGREDIENTS

4 ounces Green Beans, ends snipped off
Garlic Clove, sliced thinly
1½ tablespoons Olive Oil
1 tablespoon Crushed Red Pepper
1 tablespoon Reduced Fat Grated Parmesan
Juice of ¼ of an Orange

DIRECTIONS

Microwave Green Beans for 3 minutes or until cooked but still crunchy.

Mix all other ingredients in a bowl.

Add Green Beans and toss in mixture.

Serve with as a side with Lunch.

HIPPIE WEDGE

Period cookbooks, old newspapers, and culinary reference books confirm the popularity of iceberg (also known as Crisphead) lettuce in the 1920s. They do not, however, reveal claimants (hotels, chefs, restaurants) to the invention of the classic American wedge-type salad served with creamy dressing. The general concensus of current sources squarely places this salad as a ubiquitous menu entry of the 1950s and 1960s. The lettuce wedge lost its place in the 1970s when consumers were intrigued by more interesting salads. Recently, the iceberg wedge salad has resurfaced as a "reinvented" item on trendy menus.

INGREDIENTS

1/6 head of Iceberg Lettuce, in Wedge form
1/2 Roma Tomato, seeded and chopped
1/6 small Red Onion, chopped
1/4 Avocado, peeled and chopped
1 piece of Low Fat Swiss Cheese, chopped
2 tablespoons low Sodium Balsamic Vinaigrette

DIRECTIONS

Plate the Iceberg Wedge.

Top with Tomato, Onion and Avocado.

Finish off with Swiss cheese.

Pour dressing over wedge and serve as a side dish.

Add Ground Black Pepper if desired.

STRAWBERRY GREENS FOREVER

The word strawberry comes from the Old English streawberige, most likely because the plant sends out runners which could be likened to pieces of straw. Strawberries are native to North America, and the Indians used them in many dishes. The first colonists in America shipped the native larger strawberry plants back to Europe as early as 1600. Another variety was also discovered in Central and South America, which the conquistadors called futilla. Early Americans did not bother cultivating strawberries, because they were abundant in the wilds.

INGREDIENTS

6 ounces Baby Greens
6 Strawberries, sliced
½ Avocado, peeled and sliced
¼ cup Unsalted Pecans, chopped
1 tablespoon Olive Oil
1 tablespoon White Sugar
2 teaspoons Honey
1½ teaspoons Cider Vinegar
½ teaspoon Lemon juice

DIRECTIONS

In a bowl, whisk together Sugar, Oil, Honey, Vinegar and Lemon Juice.

Plate Greens and top with Avocado and Strawberries.

Pour dressing over salad then sprinkle with Pecans.

Refrigerate for an hour and then enjoy.

A LITTLE ON THE SIDE SALAD

Romaine or cos lettuce is a variety of lettuce which grows in a tall head of sturdy leaves with a firm rib down the center. Unlike most lettuces, it is tolerant of heat. Many dictionaries trace the word cos to the name of the Greek island of Cos, from which the lettuce was presumably introduced. It apparently reached the West via Rome, as in Italian it is called lattuga romana and in French laitue romaine.

INGREDIENTS

4 ounces Romaine or Baby Greens
4 slices of Cucumber, quartered
10 slices of Mushrooms
4 Cherry Tomatoes, halved
⅛ Red Onion, chopped
2 tablespoons low-sodium Balsamic Vinaigrette

DIRECTIONS

Place lettuce on plate.

Add all other ingredients except for dressing.

Top with Vinaigrette.

Serve as a side or double ingredients and serve as a meal.

SOME SALADS & SOME SIDES

THE ANTI-TRADITIONAL PASTO

Antipasto (plural antipasti) means "before the meal" and is the traditional first course of a formal Italian meal. The contents of an antipasto vary greatly according to regional cuisine. It is quite possible to find in the south of Italy different preparations of saltwater fish and traditional southern cured meats (like soppressata), whereas in northern Italy it will contain different kinds of cured meats and mushrooms and probably, especially near lakes, preparations of freshwater fish. The cheeses included also vary significantly between regions and backgrounds.

INGREDIENTS

Can no salt added Tuna, drained
7 ounces bagged Iceberg/Romaine or Lettuce of choice
4 ounces Low Sodium Kidney Beans, drained
¼ Red Bell Pepper, seeded and diced
⅛ Red Onion, finely chopped
1 ounce Swiss cheese, shredded
4 tablespoons Lemon Juice
2 tablespoons Olive Oil
1 tablespoon Parsley
Black Pepper

DIRECTIONS

Combine Beans, Tuna, Bell Pepper, Onion, Cheese, Parsley, 2 Tablespoon Lemon Juice and 1 Tablespoon Oil in a bowl.

Pour the remaining Lemon Juice and Oil in another bowl. Add Lettuce and toss to coat.

Plate the Lettuce and top with Tuna mixture.

Add Black Pepper.

SHRIMP J. COBB SALAD

Various stories of how the traditional Cobb salad was invented exist. One says that it came about in the 1930s at the Hollywood Brown Derby restaurant, where it became a signature dish. It is named for the restaurant's owner, Robert Howard Cobb. Stories vary as to whether the salad was invented by Cobb or by his chef, Chuck Wilson. The legend is that Cobb had not eaten until near midnight, and so he mixed together leftovers he found in the kitchen, along with some bacon cooked by the line cook, and tossed it with their French dressing.

INGREDIENTS

6 ounces bagged chopped Romaine Hearts
5 grape or cherry tomatoes
¼ Cucumber, sliced
4 ounces pre-cooked Shrimp
1 hard-boiled Egg, sliced
2 tablespoons low sodium Vinaigrette dressing
Ground Pepper

DIRECTIONS

Combine Romaine, Tomatoes, Cucumber, Shrimp and Eggs in a bowl.

Add pepper to taste.

Pour in dressing and toss.

Serve.

SOME SALADS & SOME SIDES

BALL O CASSAVA

Cassava was a staple food for pre-Columbian peoples in the Americas and is often portrayed in indigenous art. The Moche people often depicted yuca in their ceramics. Since being introduced by Portuguese traders from Brazil in the 16th century, maize and cassava have replaced traditional African crops as the continent's most important staple food crops. Cassava is sometimes described as the 'bread of the tropics but should not be confused with the tropical and equatorial bread tree, the breadfruit or the African breadfruit . People mistakenly call it Yucca.

INGREDIENTS

½ pound Boiled Cassava (Yuca)
¼ cup Cream
¼ cup shredded mozzarella
¼ cup low sodium bread crumbs
Olive Oil

DIRECTIONS

Preheat pan with oil at medium heat.

Mash Cassava until it becomes pasty.

In a bowl add cream and mozzarella to the paste.

Mold into 6 small balls and slightly flatten.

Sprinkle each one with bread crumbs.

Fry for 3 minutes on each side, until the outside turns golden.

Remove from pan and place on paper towels to absorb oil.

Serve with cooked green or red peppers.

SOUPY KALES

Soup is considered to be as old as the history of cooking. In times when food was scarce, dumping various **ingredients** into a pot to boil was not only cheap, it was filling. Its simple constitution made it accessible to rich and poor alike, and simple **ingredients** made it easy to digest for the both the healthy and sick. Each culture adopted its own variation with the **ingredients** on hand—Spanish gazpacho, Russian borscht, Italian minestrone—but the basics remain the same. Watery gruel is the likeliest origin of soup. Cereals would be roasted and ground into a paste, which would later be cooked. The word "soup" probably derives from the bread over which this gruel was poured, called a "sop" or "sup."

INGREDIENTS

¼ lb. Kale stems removed
¼ Onion, chopped
1 cup of Water
Black Pepper
Olive Oil
½ 14.5 ounce can of Low-Sodium Cannellini or White Beans, drained
½ cup low-sodium Chicken Broth

DIRECTIONS

In a medium sauce pan heat Olive Oil over medium-high heat. Add Onion and cook for 5 minutes.

Add half of the beans and slightly mash with a fork.

Add water and stock and bring to a boil.

Stir in kale, remaining beans and black pepper.

Partially cover, reduce heat and simmer until Kale is tender, about 20 minutes.

Ladle into a bowl and serve with some low-sodium crackers.

SOME SALADS & SOME SIDES

NOW THAT'S A PEAR!

USA Pears are grown in Oregon and Washington where the right mix of volcanic soil, clean mountain water and warm spring and summer days, with cool nights, combine to produce some of the world's finest pears. Oregon and Washington produce 84% of the nation's fresh pear crop. Only pears grown in Oregon and Washington are sold under the USA Pears label and they are a unique fruit in that they ripen best off the tree. As such pears are transported when they're fully mature, but not always ripe. This assures that pears you buy are in good condition to properly ripen them at home after you buy them.

INGREDIENTS

6 ounces bagged Baby Spinach
½ Pear, cored and sliced
2 tablespoons crumbled Blue Cheese
1 tablespoon chopped Red Onion
2 teaspoons water
1.5 teaspoons Red Wine Vinegar
1 teaspoon Olive Oil
1 teaspoon Honey
1 teaspoon Dijon Mustard
Black Pepper

DIRECTIONS

In a small bowl, mix together water, vinegar, olive oil, honey, Dijon mustard and black pepper.

In a large bowl add pear slices and a ⅓ of the vinaigrette and toss to coat.

Add spinach, onion and remaining dressing and toss.

Made in the USA
Lexington, KY
13 January 2016